Songwriting

The Words, the Music and the Money

Second Edition

Dick Weissman

Hal Leonard Books
An Imprint of Hal Leonard Corporation

Hal Leonard Books

An Imprint of Hal Leonard Corporation

7777 West Bluemound Road

Milwaukee, WI 53213

Trade Book Division Editorial Offices

33 Plymouth St., Montclair, NJ 07042

Second edition published in 2010. First edition published in 2001.

Printed in the United States of America

Book design by Lisa Vaughn, Two of Cups Design Studio, Inc.

Library of Congress Cataloging-in-Publication Data

Weissman, Dick.

Songwriting : the words, the music & the money / Dick Weissman. — 2nd ed.

     p. cm.

Includes bibliographical references and index.

   ISBN 978-1-4234-8451-6

1. Popular music—Writing and publishing. 2. Music—Instruction and study. I. Title.

   MT67.W362 2010

   782.42164'13—dc22

                                                        2010039288

www.halleonard.com

CONTENTS

There are quite a few books on the market that discuss songwriting. The purpose of this book is to discuss songwriting in a realistic and intelligent way without making any assumptions that one particular style of song is superior to another. I also have no particular feelings about the validity of songs. If you want to write songs that reflect your deepest feelings or thoughts, what you end up with may or may not be commercially viable. Nothing says that a commercial song can't be heartfelt and intelligent. On the other hand, nothing says that commercial songs must be particularly brilliant or innovative from the standpoint of lyrics, melodies or rhythms. Popular songs are so inextricably tied to aspects of production and performance that it is often difficult to separate the underlying song from these elements.

This is the first book about songwriting to be accompanied by a CD that covers most of the musical concepts discussed in the book itself. The CD includes both raw and finished performances and examples of melody and lyric writing. We will look at the different mannerisms that define various musical styles, and the CD will provide examples of songs, written by me and by others, that represent different musical genres.

Our discussions of the business of songwriting and music publishing are designed to help the aspiring songwriter find ways of getting songs performed and recorded by other artists.

I have been writing songs and instrumental music for many years. A number of my compositions have been recorded by artists in various styles. Songwriting is an interesting and entertaining pursuit. This book is designed to help you improve your songs, and to encourage you to continue to write them.

Thanks to the people at Hal Leonard Corporation for their help in getting this project off the ground. Thanks also to the students at the Denver Children's Home and the University of Colorado at Denver for sharing their songs and putting up with my critiques. Over the years I have been deeply influenced by the songs of Curtis Mayfield and Joni Mitchell. Thanks to Grant Landsbach, Jim Mason and Tony Rosario for permission to use their work, and to Fred Ahlert for permission to print "Blind Gary," "The Eye That Never Sleeps," and "Won't You Come with Me."

For this revised edition of the book, we have added a video, which shows two actual song collaborations.

Anyone Can Write a Song

I honestly believe that anyone can write a song. Most little children write songs all the time. They sing them in cars, at home and when they are playing. Somehow many of us are taught that we can't write songs, that it takes some sort of individual who has special training. In the same way we tend to disbelieve that we can draw or paint, or even act. In many cultures it is the norm for people to dance, sing and create music and art. In Western society we have turned these endeavors into "professional" tasks. Consequently, many people grow up denying the possibility of their own creativity.

I have written songs with children ranging in age from elementary school to junior high. I have taught songwriting at colleges and summer workshops, and to business executives taking creativity workshops in the hopes of bringing new ways of thinking back to their corporate lives. I have also taught songwriting to senior citizens.

When I say that anyone can write a song, I literally mean anyone. Most people's reaction to this will be one of skepticism: "I've never even written a poem…I can't even play a musical instrument…I can't sing…I don't have anything to say." I maintain that it really doesn't make any difference. In the next chapter we will look into where song ideas originate. In the following chapters we will explore the history of popular songs and the structure of songs.

I don't believe that it is possible to teach anyone to write brilliant songs. I think an exploration of existing popular music can give you indicators of how hit songs are written. I can't promise that when you finish this book you will be able to write commercially successful songs.

What I can offer you is the assurance that when you finish this book you will know more about songwriting than when you started it. Whether this will affect the way you work only you can tell.

Getting Started

WHICH COMES FIRST, THE WORDS OR THE MUSIC?

Beginning songwriters always want to know whether the words are written before the music, or if the music should come first. There is no definitive way that songwriters work. The ultimate answer probably depends upon an objective assessment of your strengths and weaknesses as a writer. If the ideas are easy for you but developing melodies is not, then it is logical to begin with the lyrics.

If melodies come easier to you than lyrics, then it is logical to begin your songs by writing the melodies. It is even possible, especially in writing songs where rhythm is the most important ingredient in the mix, to start the song with some sort of rhythmic figure or groove.

Other writers begin with a concept or a central idea that will influence the direction of the song. They may then write a melody that embodies that concept, and write the rest of the song later. Many songwriters walk around with notebooks filled with song ideas, or make tapes that contain melodic fragments. They use these notebooks or tapes as a kind of reference, and either return to them when looking for ideas for songs or consult them when

they are trying to finish one that is partially completed. Oftentimes a writer will write a complete song that he or she will then decide is not strong enough as a whole. Nevertheless, the song may contain a single line, phrase or chorus that survives self-critical scrutiny. The hope is that the writer will later incorporate this fragment into a new song.

There is a school of thought that believes that if a song or lyric is really a good one, you will remember it. Many writers disagree with this notion. In today's complex world of email and cell phones, there are constant distractions that can lead to a loss of concentration or memory. Some writers utilize answering machines or cell phones, and record fragments of ideas by singing them into these devices. It's more a matter of individual taste and working methods, rather than an iron-clad method of working. It's also true that some people have much better memories than others. Writing down or recording your song ideas is a way of protecting yourself. There's plenty of time later to determine whether you think that the original ideas is worthwhile.

Many writers are significantly stronger at one part of the songwriting process than the other; some are better lyricists, others better melodists. In such cases a writer will often seek to find a collaborator who is strong in the area that complements his or her own weakness. When collaborators work together they may write the words and music simultaneously, or one writer may come up with a complete melody (or lyric), leaving the other writer to write the lyric (or melody). Some writers work best when they are together, working off each other's energy and ideas, while others prefer to work alone and get together with their cowriter simply to do final rewrites.

This has been a rather elaborate way of saying that there isn't any simple answer to the question of whether the lyrics or the melody comes first. It is entirely dependent upon the writer's skills or moods. When writers feel that they are in a rut, or experiencing "writer's block," they are apt to change their usual method of working. Under those circumstances a person who typically writes the lyrics first might deliberately start with the melody.

Some older songwriters deliberately look for younger writers to work with because they are more familiar with current colloquial expressions, or rhythms and chord progressions that may be in vogue. Most sixty-year-old writers do not hang out with teenagers, and don't speak the language of young people. For the younger writer, the benefit of such a collaboration is to utilize the experience, reputation and contacts that an older writer has developed over the years.

DIFFERENCES BETWEEN SONGS AND POEMS

Although there are some similarities between poems and the lyrics of songs, poetry and song are quite different from one another. First of all, poetry usually has a formality of language that would appear incongruous in popular songs. No songwriter would use language like "To thine own self be true," but they might express the same sentiment in a more accessible way, as John Phillips did in his song "Go Where You Want to Go."

There is also a difference in the way rhymes are used in song as opposed to poems. Outside of modern-day poetry "slams," where public performance is the writer's primary outlet, poems need to work on the page. In other words, poems are generally meant to be *read,* songs are usually *sung.* I had a student who rhymed the words "Cleveland" and "evenin'." This looks awkward when written on a page, but it worked perfectly well when she rapped the lyric. She pronounced Cleveland as "Clevelin'," which made the rhyme work. In general songwriters take liberties with the English language that traditional poets would tend to frown upon. This is particularly true of rap and country songs, where the use of colloquial expressions or pronunciations unknown in high school English classes are typical.

Look at this in another way. Imagine how the songs of Ray Charles look on paper. He can take a simple element, like the word "ooh," and turn it into many syllables. In one instance he may sing it as oo-ooo-oo-oo-h. He may sing the phrase later with fewer or more syllables. Except in rare instances, poets don't improvise lyrics, and they don't change the length of syllables.

Poetry may be directly accessible to the reader or it may involve the use of abstractions, in a sort of intellectual puzzle. Rarely do poets use non-words simply for their sound value. Phrases like "da do ron ron" or "ooh shooby do" come to mind. No one listening to a song with these phrases thinks that they actually mean anything. They are simply ear candy, syllables that stick in the listener's mind because of their uniqueness. Certain songwriters have a particular gift for making up words that manage to convey their meaning anyway. An example of this sort of writing is Laura Nyro's phrase "surry on down," in the song "Stone Soul Picnic," which uses a catchy made-up word suggesting "let's hurry" that, when repeated, becomes a memorable part of the song.

It is true that certain lyrics may stand up on the printed page as poetry. In fact, a number of books have collected song lyrics in written form. Writers like Joni Mitchell and Curtis Mayfield use colorful words in a symbolic or visual manner that parallels the way poets write. Because they write memorable melodies, the listener is more likely to remember these phrases.

WRITING ALONE OR WITH COLLABORATORS

If you are intimidated by the process of songwriting, or lack confidence in your ability to complete the words and music to a song, then it is a good idea to find a writing partner. Where can you find a collaborator? Most large cities have songwriting organizations, many of which are listed in the appendix of this book. By joining these organizations and attending meetings you will find other people who are looking for a collaborator.

If there is no songwriting organization in your town, you can put up a notice at local music stores or college music departments, or ask any of the local music teachers if they know of anyone who wants to work with another writer. Other sources of collaboration may include any social group that you belong to, whether it's a sports club, a church, a YMCA or any kind of social organization. The American Federation of Musicians has several hundred local offices throughout the United States and Canada. Their members are professional musicians, some of whom are full-time musicians, while others are part-timers.

Another source of collaborators is people who are already involved in performing. They may be soloists or people in bands. The advantage of working with someone who performs regularly is that you may hear your songs performed in public and judge how people react to your work. There is also a possibility that these performers may eventually record your songs. If you are especially fortunate, that

in turn may bring your songs to a broad audience and become a source of income for you.

Record producers, especially successful ones, are another source of collaborators. Record producers obviously have access to artists who are recording, and they also may have a good idea of what a particular artist looks for in a song.

WHO DOES WHAT IN A COLLABORATION?

The question of what to look for depends to a considerable extent on an assessment of your own skills and weaknesses. If you are a strong lyricist but weaker at coming up with melodies, then obviously you are looking for someone with musical skills. If you are a singer but don't play any musical instruments, a collaborator who does play an instrument may provide you with a way of arranging your songs that is playable by other musicians.

If you are able to come up with interesting melodies without much trouble, you probably will be looking for someone who is fluent at writing lyrics. You may find that crafting melodies to specific lyrics will stimulate you to examine your melodies more closely. Writing tunes to lyrics requires more discipline and organization than the act of simply writing melodies. If you listen closely to popular songs you will notice that very few songs have identical melodies from verse to verse. Working with a lyricist will increase your awareness of how to come up with slight variations on your melodies.

Some people need a collaborator as a source of energy and discipline. It is a lot easier to goof off if you are the only person working on a project. My friend John Phillips, founder of the Mamas and Papas, used to like to stay up all night working on new songs. He was a very intense person, with a low threshold for boredom. In order to keep himself focused on a task, he would offer a share of his songs to someone whose basic function was to keep him company and act as a sounding board for his many ideas. This may seem strange, but it probably was a good investment on John's part, because he has certainly written more than his share of hit songs (such as "California Dreamin'," "Monday Monday," "Creeque Alley," "Kokomo," etc., etc.).

DEVELOPING A WORKING RELATIONSHIP WITH A COLLABORATOR

When two writers get together in a fruitful collaboration, there is an indefinable energy in the room as they bounce ideas off one another. This is the typical method of collaboration in Nashville. The writers make a formal appointment, and begin either with an idea that one of the writers has or by picking up guitars and starting to play little rhythmic or melodic figures.

Successful collaborations involve many aspects of personal and musical style. For example, some people work best in the morning, others at night. If the collaboration consists of working together in the same room, one person is going to have to compromise. But beyond the time of day, writers have different styles of developing a song. Some people have ideas that come in rapid bursts like machine gun fire, one after the other in quick succession. Others are more reflective and prefer to spend some time thinking about a song before writing.

As you will see in more detail when we discuss how melodies are written, some people hear melodies in their head, others derive them from experimenting with chord progressions. Some people need to be playing an instrument to write, others hum or whistle, and prefer *not* to have an instrument in their hands.

If you are planning to collaborate here is a checklist of things to look for:

1) **Are your tastes and styles compatible?**

If you are going to write together there should be a maximum of work and a minimum of arguments at your sessions.

2) **Are your personal styles suitable to working together?**

This involves not only matters like what time of day you like to work, but the length of time that writing sessions last and the amount of rewriting that you are willing to commit to doing. You also should find a mutually compatible workplace.

3) **Do you like one another?**

Cowriters needn't be close friends, but they should at least have some degree of mutual respect. Failing that, they are not likely to listen to each other's ideas.

4) **Are your goals similar?**

If you are not after the same goals, there can't be the sort of appropriate teamwork and cooperation that results in the successful (and happy) completion of a song.

5) **Do the two writers have skills that complement one another?**

If both writers are skilled at writing lyrics but weak at creating melodies, collaboration is probably a foolish venture.

5) **The greed factor:**

If you are going to work with someone on any kind of regular basis, the two of you should have a good feeling about what each person is contributing. If your cowriter wants to apportion each song differently, say one on a 60-40 basis, another on a 75-25 basis, then you are probably not going to have a long and fruitful collaboration.

Keep in mind that collaboration can involve more than two people. It is not unusual for bands to try to write songs together. Often this results in some confusion about the songwriting process. Coming up with a bass part is not really part of writing a song, unless you can honestly say that the song could not exist without that bass part. For this reason, bands that start out trying to write songs together often conclude that one, two or three of the band members are the real songwriters. When we talk about the financial aspects of songwriting and publishing you will see how it is possible for all members of a group to share in the music publishing rights of a band's songs.

There are compelling reasons to collaborate when writing songs, and there are good reasons not to. It is a matter of style, experience and talent. Ultimately only you can judge what is best. It is a good idea to attempt to collaborate, even if you don't plan to often write with other songwriters. It will give you a feel for the way other people approach the art.

Many writers work with a variety of collaborators. One collaboration may work because of mutual interests, while another might work for exactly the opposite reason, with each writer thinking, "I never would have thought of that."

CHAPTER 1 RESOURCES

There is actually an entire book on collaboration. It is Walter Carter's *The Songwriter's Guide to Collaboration*, published by Writer's Digest. This may be more information than you need, but if you have never collaborated before, it is a worthwhile reference.

The DVD that comes with this book is another resource that can help you understand how collaboration works.

Form and a Bit of History

THE DEVELOPMENT OF POPULAR SONGS

The first American who seems to have seen himself as a professional songwriter as opposed to a performer who also wrote songs was Stephen Foster. Foster was able to make a modest living by convincing minstrel companies to perform his songs. He sold some songs for a flat fee, without the payment of royalties. There were other cases where Foster retained his rights as a composer and received royalties. Unfortunately Foster's tangled personal life and alcoholism often caused him to sell songs outright in order to survive. Foster was not a performer, teacher or church musician, so I guess we could call him the first professional American songwriter. George Root was another early composer who received royalty payments.

Through the 1920s the basic goal of songwriters was to get performers to feature their songs. This happened at vaudeville shows, cabarets and theaters. It was not unusual for songwriters and/or publishers to pay performers to feature their songs. Sometimes payments were made in cash, and sometimes the performer was cut in on the copyright of a song.

The primary source of income for songwriters who were able to obtain royalty deals was through the sale of sheet music. Often the sheet music had the picture of the performer who was featuring the song on the cover. Kerry Segrave's fascinating book *Payola in the Music Industry*[1] tells of all sorts of bribes that were given to assist in popularizing songs. These included payoffs to performers and hiring people to cheer when songs were featured in shows or nightclub acts. Free copies of the sheet music and even orchestrations were provided to bandleaders and vocalists. Song pluggers who worked for music publishers would sometimes hand out copies of the words of new songs to patrons of cafés or saloons, so that the audience could sing along with the performer. This practice was designed to create an aura of enthusiasm for the song that would further entice the performer to keep using it in his act. According to Segrave, the songwriters in the 1890s typically received a royalty of 4 percent of the net receipts of the sales of the sheet music. Repeated performances of the songs would stimulate the audiences to purchase the sheet music, much as repeated plays of a song on the radio today will induce people to buy the recording. In 1891 international copyright protection was legislated, so that an English composer's music was protected in America and vice versa.

My mother was brought up in New York City and was an amateur singer and piano player. She told me that the way she learned new material in the1920s and 1930s was through song pluggers who performed new songs in five-and-dime stores. This attracted a crowd of customers eager to hear the latest hits. She, along with the others, would then buy the songs that she liked.

Another method of circulating new songs was via Broadway shows. Segrave reports numerous instances where publishers utilized some form of bribe to ensure that key songs made their way into specific shows. Publishers eventually rebelled against the practice of payola by forming an organization called the Music Publishers' Protective Association. By 1917 most publishers had joined this organization, and they were successful in limiting the practice of payola.

Initially, songwriters and publishers did not receive royalties from recordings. A court test by the music publishers was unsuccessful, but publishers then lobbied amateur songwriters to bombard Congress with letters demanding royalty payments to songwriters on record sales. This campaign proved successful, and the Copyright Act of 1909 established a two-cent royalty for each copy of a record sold. It also initiated the practice of compulsory licenses, which still exists today. Under these licenses, once a song has been recorded, other artists can record the song too, as long as they agree to pay the requisite royalties. Then, as now, it was also possible to negotiate payments smaller than the payments set forth in the act.

In 1914, ASCAP, the American Society of Composers, Authors and Publishers, was formed. The oft-told story of its formation maintains that composer Victor Herbert became incensed when he heard his tunes being performed in cafés without any payment to him. It wasn't until the 1920s that ASCAP was able to win a lawsuit that enabled publishers and songwriters to collect performance rights from radio airplay of records.

TIN PAN ALLEY

Nineteenth-century sheet music was published in various places. Most of Scott Joplin's ragtime compositions were published by John Stark in Sedalia, Missouri. By the beginning of the twentieth century New York had become the capital of music publishing. Music publishers, song pluggers and songwriters were mostly located in the Union Square section of Manhattan. By 1900 most of these publishers had moved to West 28th Street, between Broadway and Fifth Avenue. The area was immortalized in 1903 when a songwriter and journalist named Morris Rosenfeld visited a music publisher's office on the street. The publisher wound strips of paper around the piano strings to produce a tinny sound that he enjoyed. Rosenfeld used that sound as the basis for his article, which he entitled "Tin Pan Alley." This became the name of both the street and the songwriting tradition that sprung from it. Such famous songwriters as Irving Berlin and George M. Cohan rose to fame there.

ON BROADWAY

Broadway shows in the 1920s included a number of musical revues by black composers such as Will Marion Cook, J. Rosamond Johnson, Eubie Blake and Noble Sissle. In the 1930s the Broadway musical developed into a more mainstream genre with white composers like Richard Rodgers, Lorenz Hart, Jerome Kern and Cole Porter. This style of sophisticated, almost cabaret-oriented music held strong through the 1950s and into the 1960s.

Some Broadway shows, such as *Oklahoma!*, literally ran for years at a stretch. They were also performed around the country in regional productions, as well as at colleges and high schools. Some of these shows were also done as Hollywood musicals, generating further revenue for the writers and publishers.

Many of these shows continue to generate revenue through

revivals. Broadway revivals not only result in revenue from ticket sales, they also renew interest in old and new recordings of shows. This leads to more dinner theater and school performances.

BMI, ROCK 'N' ROLL AND THE RISE OF COUNTRY MUSIC

In 1939 radio stations rebelled against ASCAP's attempts to increase the fees that stations had to pay in order to license music for airplay. The broadcasters formed their own performing rights association, BMI (Broadcast Music Incorporated). Since ASCAP had a lock on almost all of the current songwriters, BMI looked around for forms of music that ASCAP was ignoring at the time. ASCAP had pretty much been the citadel of the old-time Tin Pan Alley and Broadway songwriters, and had not welcomed other forms of music into the organization. Country music, for example, was sneered at as an indicator of musical illiteracy. BMI shrewdly welcomed blues, country music and jazz composers and songwriters into the fold.

The formation of BMI in 1940 corresponded almost exactly with the increasing popularity of rhythm and blues, a sort of big-city version of traditional blues music. New markets were created overnight that valued styles of music ASCAP had scorned.

Rock 'n' roll became popular in the mid-1950s. During this period, BMI had a virtual lock on the pop charts as ASCAP continued to ignore "semi-literate" musicians and musical styles.

Eventually ASCAP realized that rock 'n' roll and country music were not going to go away, and today writers of all genres belong to one or the other of the performing rights societies, or to a third, much smaller, organization called SESAC.

SONGWRITER-RECORDING ARTISTS

Most early rock artists, outside of Chuck Berry and Buddy Holly, did not write their own music. They relied on a group of younger songwriter-record producers for their material. By the mid-1960s Bob Dylan and the Beatles had created an environment where recording artists began to write a large percentage of their own music. Some artists, like Paul Simon, never record songs that they do not write. Today a majority of pop music artists write or cowrite their own songs. Nevertheless, there are still artists like Whitney Houston, Linda Ronstadt, Celine Dion, Reba McEntire and a large number of country and western performers who write little or none of their own music. There are also teams of songwriter-producers like Max Martin in Sweden, and Stock Aitken Waterman in England, or The Neptunes in Virginia Beach, who function as both songwriters and producers for a variety of artists. As we will see later on in this book, the opportunities for songwriters are narrower than they were a hundred years ago, but burgeoning new outlets such as cable television, CD-ROM, movies and the internet are lucrative sources of potential income.

CHAPTER 2 RESOURCES

Footnote 1: Kerry Seagrave's *Payola In The Music Industry, A History, 1880-1991*, published by McFarland and Co., Jeffersons, N.C., 1994. See pages 1-8.

David Jasen's and Gene Jone's *Spreadin' Rhythm Around: Black Popular Songwriters, 1880-1930,* published by Schirmer Books, 1998, is an interesting history of a little-known phenomenon.

Prince Dorough's book *Popular Music Culture In America,* N.Y., Ardley House, 1992, relates the Rosenfeld story.

The Form of Popular Music

THE A FORM

The simplest songs utilize a single form, sometimes called the A form. This indicates that there is a single melody used throughout the song. There are two sorts of songs that are constructed in this fashion: traditional ballads (songs that tell a story) and children's songs.

Traditional folk ballads were written in this way because the center of a "performance" is the lyric of the song. The singer is simply seen as the vehicle for transmitting the story. By utilizing a single melody, there are no distractions for the listener. One such style of songs exists in the traditional Serbian ballads about the defeat of the Serbs by the Turks at the battle of Kosovo in the fourteenth century. Some of these Serbian heroic ballads are over a hundred verses long.

English ballads are a somewhat more modest representation of the same sort of song. "Pretty Polly," a sixteenth-century English-Scottish murder ballad, is an example. It starts off like this:

I courted pretty Polly, all the livelong night,
Courted pretty Polly, all the livelong night,
I left her next morning, before it was light.

The song continues with the story of how the "hero" leads his pregnant girlfriend to a remote spot and then proceeds to murder her. In the early days of country music, such ballads were performed by a solo singer, either a cappella (without accompaniment) or accompanying himself on a banjo or fiddle. I have one record of "Pretty Polly" where the singer breaks up the song by playing the melody on the banjo between each of the many verses. This is a sort of extreme example of an A form, verse-only song.

Other examples of such songs that may be more familiar to the reader include "Down in the Valley" and "On Top of Old Smoky." Children's songs are often A form songs, because very small children will have an easier time remembering a single melody than having to recall two different ones. An example of an A form children's song is "Go Tell Aunt Rhody":

Go tell Aunt Rhody,
Go tell Aunt Rhody,
Go tell Aunt Rhody,
That the old gray goose is dead.
The one she's been saving,
The one she's been saving,
The one she's been saving,
To make a featherbed.

Traditional blues songs often have a verse with no chorus, and sometimes even relatively modern blues songs utilize this structure. Blues often have short instrumental figures called "turnarounds" after each verse. These turnarounds tend to mask the repetition that is inherent in verse-only songs. This is particularly important in blues, because their structure, much like that of "Aunt Rhody," contains one or two repetitions in the verses themselves. A typical blues might go like this:

> If you see me coming, hoist your window high,
> Yes if you see me coming, hoist your window high
> And if you see me leaving, hang your head and cry.

This verse is followed by an instrumental turnaround, and then another verse is sung:

> If you think you're lucky, count the days I'm gone,
> Yeah if you believe you're lucky, count the days I'm gone,
> Better teach yourself to sing some other song.

Although A form songs rarely become hits, the following are exceptions during the last thirty years:

- "Buy for Me the Rain," performed by the Nitty Gritty Dirt Band
- "The Wreck of the Edmund Fitzgerald," written and performed by Gordon Lightfoot
- "I Was Made to Love Her," written and performed by Stevie Wonder
- "Gentle on My Mind," written by John Hartford, performed by Glen Campbell
- "Scarborough Fair," traditional folk song, arranged and adapted by Simon & Garfunkel

PROS AND CONS OF THE A FORM

The biggest drawback to the A form is that it can be boring. The longer the song, the harder it is to sustain it with a single melody. It is possible to mask the repetition through an interesting instrumental arrangement or by using sophisticated production techniques. This is exactly what Lightfoot did with "The Wreck of the Edmund Fitzgerald." Each verse brought in new instruments, and this "layering" tended to make listeners forget that they were listening to the same melody over and over again.

In the case of the Stevie Wonder song, he sang the phrase "Hey, hey, hey" with a slightly different melody after each verse.

The strength of the A form is that its directness makes it memorable. Some melodies are strong enough that you don't mind hearing them over and over, and actually gain momentum from repetition, becoming almost hypnotic. Such songs are often so simple that virtually anyone can learn to sing them without much effort. Obviously, with children's music, this is desirable. In the case of blues and ballads, the performer has to rely on the strength of the story being told to hold the listener's attention. As blues bands have added more and more instruments, instrumental solos can provide some relief from the boredom of repetition.

MODIFICATIONS OF THE A FORM: THE REFRAIN AND THE HOOK

A refrain is a line that is repeated throughout a song. It differs from the chorus because the chorus does not consist of a single line or phrase, but usually contains approximately four lines of lyric and melody. The refrain is a way of dealing with the monotony of A form songs. Because the line is repeated, it tends to stay in the listener's memory. A lyric, melody or melodic figure that sticks in the listener's memory is referred to as a *hook*. Catchy or memorable song titles can also be hooks.

An example of an A form with a hook is Jerry Jeff Walker's song "Mr. Bojangles." At the end of the verse, Walker repeats the phrase "Mr. Bojangles." Since "Mr. Bojangles" is also the title of the song, and describes a colorful and interesting figure, this provides the extra bit of spice that makes the otherwise pedestrian A form work.

Pete Seeger's song "Where Have All the Flowers Gone," popularized by the Kingston Trio, is an A form song. The title phrase is repeated numerous times in the song, but it is an unusual enough phrase to keep the listener interested in the song.

Another variation on the A form can be found in a song I wrote called "Someone to Talk My Troubles To." The title is the refrain, which varies from the lyric "no one to talk my troubles to," but the song has no chorus and features a separate bridge.

If you want to write an A form song, you must be aware of the dangers of repetition. You therefore need to modify the form in a creative way. As explained above, that can be through the use of an especially unusual lyric line that is repeated in the song, or by using a refrain. You may be able to write a song whose melody or story line is so incredibly riveting that the listener is unaware of the repetitive nature of the tune.

EXAMPLES
- "The Way We Were," words by Alan and Marilyn Bergman, music by Marvin Hamlish, performed by Barbara Streisand
- "Eleanor Rigby," written by John Lennon and Paul McCartney, performed by the Beatles

AB FORM, USING THE SAME MELODY FOR THE VERSE AND CHORUS

In this technique the verse and chorus have the same melody, but the chorus introduces a different lyric. The reason for using this form in the case of a children's song

is again for ease of retention. In the case of other songs, the writer may simply not have been able to come up with a better melody than the verse melody that he or she originally wrote.

EXAMPLES
- "This Land Is Your Land," written by Woody Guthrie, performed by numerous artists
- "Born in the USA," written and performed by Bruce Springsteen

AB FORM WITH DIFFERENT MELODIES

This is one of the classic forms used in popular music. Because the chorus is the part of the song that is repeated anywhere from three to five or more times, it is the chorus that usually contains the more interesting melody, and the strongest part of the lyric. Typically, although not always, it will also include the title of the song.

It is also quite common for the chorus to be sung in a higher register than the verse, and for the chorus to be sung in harmony. It is the chorus of a song that most people will remember.

The length of a song will often determine the way the verses and choruses are configured. For example, if you were to decide to write a song with six verses, it would be typical to group two verses together before each chorus. Six verses is a long song by today's standards. In more typical songs containing two or three verses, the chorus usually appears after each verse. It is also possible to start the song with a chorus. The advantage of starting with the chorus is that it immediately sets the tone of the song. It may also, however, weaken the impact of the first verse. Since it is generally the first verse that sets up the plot line of the song, this may or may not be a good idea. Occasionally a song may utilize three verses before the chorus is sung.

Don Schlitz's country classic "The Gambler," as performed by Kenny Rogers, is an example of this technique. Once again, this is a story song with a long lyric, so waiting for the chorus built suspense, and also kept the song at an attractive "radio-friendly" length. Recordings often modify song form because the artist chooses to change the way the writer has originally structured it. Nanci Griffith wrote the song "Love At the Five and Dime," and in her version she sang the chorus after the first verse. The hit version, recorded by Kathy Mattea, waited until the end of the second verse before using the chorus. This was probably done because this is a story song with a rather lengthy lyric. Griffith's decision to get to the chorus quickly is one of those odd examples where what seemed like a commercially viable way of making a record was less effective than making the audience wait for the chorus.

EXAMPLES

- "A Hard Day's Night," written by Lennon and McCartney, performed by the Beatles
- "Lean On Me," written and performed by Bill Withers
- "Because You Loved Me," written by Diane Warren, performed by Celine Dion

THE BRIDGE

The bridge introduces a new melody and lyric to the verse/chorus format. It can be used as a diversion from the central theme of a song, or to reflect a different point of view than the song has utilized up to that point. A bridge is often used when a song is (or seems) particularly long, but it can also be used simply for the sake of variety, regardless of the length. The bridge is generally found toward the end of a song, often as a substitute for the third verse.

The bridge is often followed directly by a chorus, and if there is another verse, it would then appear after that chorus. Jimmy Driftwood's "The Ballad of New Orleans" features a classic use of a bridge. This is a very long song about the last battle of the War of 1812. The melody of the verse uses the traditional fiddle tune "The Eighth of January," while the chorus uses a new melody. The bridge then is sung higher than the chorus, which almost has the effect of adding an additional chorus. Since Driftwood repeats the bridge, he was obviously aware that it was an attractive tune in its own right.

WHEN DO YOU USE A BRIDGE?

We have already discussed the use of a bridge to make long songs more interesting. It is also possible to utilize the bridge in order to develop a new point of view in a song. For example, if you were writing a song about a failed romance from the point of view of the dominant member of the relationship, the bridge might highlight the feelings of the other person in the relationship.

In the song "Take Me Home, Country Roads," written by Bill Danoff, John Denver and Taffy Nivert and recorded by John Denver, the bridge introduces the love interest in the song, which had been implied but not mentioned in the previous verses.

Bridges are often used in instrumental music, especially in jazz. In instrumental music the primary reason for using a bridge is for variety's sake. The length of the piece tends to be a secondary consideration.

EXAMPLES

- "I've Just Seen a Face," written by Lennon and McCartney, performed by the Beatles
- Verse-refrain-bridge: "I Don't Stand a Ghost of a Chance With You," written by Bing Crosby, Ned Washington & Victor Young
- "Goin' Out Of My Head," written by Teddy Randazzo and Bobby Weinstein, recorded by Little Anthony and The Imperials

THE PRE-HOOK OR CLIMB

The pre-hook or climb appears at the end of a verse, and serves as a sort of introduction to the chorus. One of the most famous uses of the climb is found in "You've Lost That Lovin' Feelin'," written by Barry Mann, Cynthia Weil and Phil Spector, and a hit twice over, first by the Righteous Brothers and later by Hall & Oates. The pre-hook is the section that starts with the lyric "It makes me feel just like cryin'."

The purpose of the pre-hook is to announce the arrival of the chorus. In order for the pre-hook or climb to work, the writer is obligated to deliver a killer chorus, or what he or she will has created is much ado about nothing.

EXAMPLES
- "Stayin' Alive," written and recorded by the Bee Gees
- "Leaving on a Jet Plane," written by John Denver, recorded by Peter, Paul & Mary

THE PROLOGUE

A prologue is an introductory bridge that was often used in popular music "standards" of the 1930s and 1940s. This introductory material is intended to set up the song, but generally does not appear in the body of the song itself. It is quite common for singers (and musicians) to simply ignore these introductory figures and go immediately to the verse of the song. Singer Johnny Mathis used to a play a game with Johnny Carson, Doc Severinsen and the musicians in the "Tonight Show" band. They would attempt to stump him by asking him to sing the intros to relatively obscure songs. Mathis seems to have an encyclopedic knowledge of these songs, and would continually astonish Carson, Severinsen and the audience.

This form has essentially been abandoned in today's music. I suppose you could look at these prologues as having the opposite effect than A form children's songs. In other words, rather than making a song easier to remember or perform, the use of these introductory melodies makes the songs more difficult to remember. Often the material introduced in the prologue is at best loosely related to the song itself. This form almost presents its lengthy introductory section as a sort of teaser to introduce the song.

EXAMPLES
- "Stardust," written by Hoagy Carmichael, performed by dozens of artists
- "Ol' Man River," written by Oscar Hammerstein II and Jerome Kern, recorded by Paul Robeson and numerous other artists

OTHER FORMS: ABCD

Under certain circumstances, it is possible to write a song that has four separate parts. At one time I was working on the music for an off-off Broadway show about Jesse James, and wrote such a song, called "Won't You Go With Me." The song was written as a duet between Jesse James and his fiancée (and eventual wife), Zerelda Mims. Each character really had his/her own song, and at the end Zerelda sang the chorus of Jesse's song with him. In this case, the form of the song could be described as ABCD, or it could be looked at as two separate songs done together as a medley, with each song in AB form. Listen to the song on the accompanying CD and it will make more sense to you. Here is the way the song is laid out:

◆1 "Won't You Go with Me"

JESSE

VERSE

If you would follow me,

I'd take you places you've never been to,

If you would follow me,

I'd show you traces you can't see alone.

CHORUS

It's always peaceful, in the valley,

And the river bend is calling,

Won't you come with me, won't you come with me, won't

you come with me.

ZERALDA'S SONG

VERSE

You know I've got my school to go to, things I never knew,

How can I be sure that I can always count on you,

CHORUS

I've got a lot of things to learn before it's time to settle

down,

And you want to make a name for yourself, and ride from

town to town.

Each singer has another verse and chorus, and then the two sing Jesse's chorus together. This device was intended to foreshadow their eventual marriage.

THROUGH-COMPOSED MUSIC

Art songs are sometimes written with no verse chorus structure. The melody is different for each new verse of the song. Many of these songs are set by composers from lyrics by trained poets, rather than songwriters. Clearly this is not a form that is not usually found in popular music, because the focus is on a performance by a trained singer, not on the listener learning the song and singing it themselves.

EXAMPLE

● "Beyond Belief" written and performed by Elvis Costello

INTROS AND INSTRUMENTAL HOOKS

Instrumental introductions are not part of the raw song itself. However, because so many songwriters play guitar or keyboard, the intros are often constructed at the same time as the song itself. In general, intros should not last for more than four or eight bars, because they are simply a device used to set up the song. There is no denying that when an audience hears a song in concert, much of the function of an intro is to enable the audience to recognize the song even before the singer starts to sing. For this reason, songwriters who have some creative skills on guitar or keyboard have a tremendous advantage over those whose playing ability is modest.

In the same way, songwriters often add little instrumental hook lines in the spaces between the lines of lyrics, or between the verse and chorus of a song. This can also be done during the verses or choruses themselves, but it is a bit tricky, because it may take the attention of the audience away from the lyric itself. The key to successful instrumental fills in the song itself is to make the hook phrases very short. This follows the old "less is more" dictum.

CHOOSING A FORM FOR YOUR SONG

Now that we have looked at most of the forms that are found in contemporary popular music, you are probably wondering how a writer goes about choosing which form to use. There isn't a simple answer to this question. It depends largely on the way the songwriter works. The "notebook writer," who carries notepads around with phrases, lines and verses, will probably choose the form from the very beginning or even before he or she starts writing.

More spontaneous writers tend to have the attitude of letting a song go wherever it seems to want to lead, and worrying about the form later. Unfortunately, sometimes when you hear a song, the author's struggles with the form are apparent. Although it is quite possible, for example, to add a bridge later on, the song should not sound as though someone has glued it together in an artificial or incongruous way.

What I am trying to say is that in the course of writing a song, the form ought to reveal itself to the writer. If a song feels long and repetitious, then a bridge is one way to solve this dilemma. If the melody of the verse seems too much like that of the chorus, then you may want to try writing a new chorus.

The question of whether or not you are concerned with having your songs be commercially successful may also play a role in determining what forms your songs take. This will involve such issues as the development of dramatic choruses, restricting the length of your songs, and developing catchy song titles and hooks.

We will go back to all of these matters as we examine the techniques of lyric and melody writing. Anyone who writes songs over a long period of time will find that repetition, staleness or a lack of inspiration are liable to set in at one time or another. Developing an understanding of different song forms, and experimenting with different styles of writing, are good ways to maintain a lifelong interest in songwriting.

CHAPTER 3 RESOURCES

There are a number of useful books about songwriting that discuss form. Besides the ones listed below, a more extensive list appears in the appendix.

Jason Blume, *6 Steps to Songwriting Success: The Comprehensive Guide to Writing and Marketing Hit Songs*, New York, Billboard Books, 1999. A useful and easy-to-read guide.

John Braheny, *The Craft and Business of Songwriting*, 3rd edition, Cincinnati, Writer's Digest Books, 2007. Braheny has an encyclopedic knowledge of songs and their construction.

Stephen Citron, *Songwriting: A Complete Guide to the Craft*, revised edition, New York, William Morrow and Co., 2008. A thorough and detailed guide.

Joel Hirschhorn. *The Complete Idiot's Guide to Songwriting*, 2nd edition, New York, Alpha, 2004. A much better book than the title implies.

Writing Lyrics

WHERE IDEAS COME FROM

One of the more obvious sources for song subjects is personal experience. Even within the context of personal experience there are decisions to be made. One way to deal with this issue is to write from your internal experiences rather than from specific events. If you write in this vein, you will be trying to transmit feelings or thought processes rather than relating literal experiences. If you are able to write in this way, you can discuss personal situations or experiences with people without creating a soap-opera approach. In an interview in Marc Woodworth's book *Solo Women Singer-Songwriters in Their Own Words,* Sarah McLachlan says that she prefers not to disclose the origins of her songs. She states, "My life is a soap opera for myself and my close friends—nobody else."

On the other hand, some writers, and certainly some fans, revel in the disclosure of personal details. So you can become the sort of writer who tells every detail of, for example, your successful or disastrous romances. You should use whatever style is comfortable for you. Performances and recordings will reveal whether audiences have any interest in these disclosures. Eric Clapton's song "Tears in Heaven" is a fairly extreme example of the sort of personal-revelation style of writing. The song is about the tragic death of his child. Whether you find such disclosures refreshingly honest or uncomfortably candid is a matter of personal taste.

Tom T. Hall has written several books about songwriting, in which he discloses that many of his songs come from observing and listening to people. This can be done at parties, bars, airports or wherever you happen to be. It is also possible to receive this sort of information from the experiences of your friends or family. Since any one person has a limited number of experiences, being aware of other people's realities is a useful source of inspiration, song titles or even entire lyrics of songs. If you move in this direction, you may want to add some details that go beyond the actual experience, in order to keep the identity of the characters in the song vague. This is particularly true when you use incidents that were disclosed to you in confidence.

Songs can also be drawn wholly from your imagination. Everyone has a greater or lesser amount of fantasy in their life. I was once on a city bus in New York, and saw a woman who was dressed in black from head to toe. I developed a series of fantasies about her, and proceeded to write a song "about" her called "The Lady in Black."

OTHER SOURCES

Books, magazine articles, television shows, comic books and theatrical performances or films are additional grist for the songwriter's personal mill. An enjoyable exercise is to watch a movie and write a song about one of the characters in the film. The lives of celebrities, whether in sports, political life or history, are another source of ideas. Newspapers and novels are other possible sources of inspiration. Personal life situations, such as the dilemma of an "old maid" ("Eleanor Rigby"), sickness, tragedy, triumph, family dramas or philosophical dilemmas are other possibilities. Particular settings like beaches, mountains, ("Rocky Mountain High"), exotic locales or unusual names of towns or countries are all possibilities. Lisa Aschmann's *500 Songwriting Ideas (For Brave and Passionate People)* can provide you with additional options if you are stuck.

GETTING STARTED

Some people start with a title or a general concept for a song. If you don't know where to start, try the following exercise. It is sometimes used in schools to help students develop ideas, and is called "webbing." In Woodworth's books on women writers, Joan Osborne says that she uses it to help her write songs.

Put your central song idea or title in the middle of a page. Associate whatever you wish with the central concept, and put these associations in writing in different parts of the page. On the next page I will do this exercise with you. I have a friend named Alex Komodore, a fine guitarist who lives in Denver. Alex is a classical guitarist, but for some time he has fantasized about writing a song around the central idea "The coffee you made for me is grounds for divorce." Put this idea in the center of your page, like this:

The coffee that you made for me is grounds for divorce

Now start to associate other ideas with this central concept. Suppose we start with the idea that a man and a woman have been married, or at least together for some time. On your empty page add the words "long-term relationship." Another association might be the idea that they have been through both good and bad times together. Your page will now look like this:

Long-term relationship. Been through a lot, good and bad.
The coffee that you made for me is grounds for divorce.

My next association is with the coffee itself: what constitutes "good" or "bad" coffee. The page now looks like this:

Good long-term relationship. Been through a lot, good
*   and bad.*
The coffee that you made for me is grounds for divorce.

Good coffee: aroma, taste, Starbucks, Maxwell House, "good to the last drop," Folger's espresso, cappucino, latte cafe, coffee house, truck stop, Peet's, Seattle's Best Vienna Roast, fresh beans, Taster's Choice, strong, wakes you up, big cup, good beans, java, cup-a-joe, smells good

Bad coffee: old, watery, bottom of the pot, weak, left on burner too long, lukewarm, stale, cold, from a greasy spoon, dump, dirty kitchen, too much sugar

This pretty much covers the coffee situation. Now let's go back and associate with the relationship.

Relationship
- Been through good and bad times, like coffee love can become lukewarm and stale, old girlfriend made great coffee and she doesn't even drink coffee. She's so spaced in the morning, she can't even make a decent cup of coffee.
- When I was younger I didn't mind going around the corner to a restaurant that made decent coffee. Coffee is a metaphor for what she won't do for me.
- We spent our honeymoon in Seattle, and I tried to

get her to like coffee. All she ever wanted to do was eat fish.

Below is the lyric that resulted from this "webbing." I have written it out in the key of D. The singer chose to do it in Bb, but D is easier to read and play on the guitar.

◆⁶ "The Coffee That You Made for Me Is Grounds for Divorce"

Words and music by Alex Komodore and Dick Weissman

VERSE

On the day that I first met you, I was barely twenty-two;
You said you really liked the things I told you I would do
We spent the early mornings at the Crocodile Cafe
Drinking lots of java at the start of every day

PRE-HOOK

We hooked up, broke up, patched up
Time and time again
Fifteen years of joy and tears
Are coming to the end

CHORUS

The coffee that you make for me is really kind of weak,
It tastes so bad, I've often had a better cup of tea;
The beans are old, the cup is cold, the taste is kind of coarse,
The coffee that you make for me is grounds for divorce.

VERSE

Our honeymoon was spent in the beautiful Northwest,
I told you in Seattle that Starbucks was the best.
You said you like the gourmet beans they
    put in a latte,
I said I like my coffee strong, that's all I
    have to say.

PRE-HOOK

We hooked up, broke up, patched up,
Time and time again.
Fifteen years of joys and tears
We're coming to the end.

CHORUS

The coffee that you make for me is really kind of weak,
It tastes so bad, I've often had a better cup of tea.
The beans are old, this coffee's cold,
    the taste is kind of harsh,
The coffee that you make for me is grounds for a divorce.

To find out how the melody of this song evolved, see the second section of this book. You can hear the song on the accompanying CD.

ANOTHER EXAMPLE OF WEBBING

This book was written in the winter of 1999-2000. Curtis Mayfield, former leader of the Impressions and a great songwriter and singer, died while the writing was in its early stages. I thought it might provide an interesting contrast to our last webbing exercise to write a tribute to Curtis, who had a very strong influence on my attitudes toward songwriting. I started off this way:

Civil rights movement, "Keep On Pushin'," "People Get Ready," coded messages, "A Movement Man," Curtis Mayfield, disco sound tracks for movies, *Superfly* "See the love in this man"

"We can deal with rockets and dreams, when it comes to
    reality, what does it mean?"
Tragedy of paralysis. Recording a song while lying down.

Since the web includes references to Curtis's career and his songs, I need to explain the references. Coded messages are lyrics with a double meaning, often found in nineteenth-century African-American spirituals. They convey one set of meanings to the average person, another to, for example, the slave seeking to escape from the plantation and his or her oppressive life.

"People Get Ready" and "Keep On Pushing" are the titles of two of the Impressions' major hit songs. Curtis's songs were adopted by the civil rights movement, and were rewritten with his permission. In the '70s he did a number of movie scores, including one to the movie *Superfly*. In the song "Freddie's Dead" he points out that there can be love even in a junkie's heart. The paralysis refers to a tragic accident where the scaffolding of an outdoor stage collapsed on Curtis, leaving him paralyzed for the remaining nine years of his life. Even in that condition he was able to write and record an album of his songs.

The phrase "Risin' Above" refers to Curtis's transcending the ghetto that he was born into. It refers to rising above one's difficulties, and also to moving to a higher place. Below is the song that came out of the exercise.

"Risin' Above"

Words and music by Dick Weissman

VERSE

Once upon a time, a man lived in Chicago,
Sending out a message to a world he grew to know
And the people, they were waiting,
For what he had to say,
Some started in to dancing, hoping he would stay

CHORUS

Risin' above, what the world has chosen for you
Risin' above, any obstacle you see,
Risin above, any harm that's meant for you,
Surrounded by love, you can rise above.

VERSE

There were so many songs, and so many stories,
Life had so many problems, and moments of glory,
He was made for the times, and society's crimes,
Melted in the visions of songs like a religion.

CHORUS

Risin' above, the road chosen for you,
Risin' above any obstacles you can see,
Risin above, any harm waitin' for you,
Surrounded by love, you can rise above

BRIDGE

Then the tragedy struck him, it couldn't
        defeat him,
He was a man with a mission, deceit wasn't in him
So he continued to write with inspiration,
Now he's honored forever, for all his creations.

CHORUS

Risin' above, the road that was chosen for him,
Risin' above, any obstacles you can see,
Risin' above, any harm that's waitin' for you,
Surrounded by love, you can rise above.

To hear how the melody for this song evolved, see the next section of this book.

PLUSES AND MINUSES OF "METHOD SONGWRITING"

It is up to the individual writer to decide whether the webbing method is useful. Some people write in a rapid-fire way, and sitting down and brainstorming word or character associations is probably disruptive to such a style. Others might use webbing, but in an entirely different way. For example, they might actually write lines in place of the associations. It is entirely up to you to decide whether you want to use any sort of predetermined method at all.

One of the best books about songwriting that I have ever seen is William Flanagan's *Written in My Soul.* In this book he interviews many songwriters. There are several other similar books. However, Flanagan seems to have an encyclopedic knowledge of songs, and he appeared to be able to get writers to trust and confide in him about their ways of writing and the various decisions they make in the course of their work. One thing that emerges repeatedly in the book is the notion that there are really two different types of writers, the "notebook" writer and the writer who sees himself as a vehicle for the transmission of songs that in effect already exist in the universe.

Paul Simon and Neil Young, both of whom are very successful writers, are probably good, if extreme, examples of the two types. Simon has many, many notebooks filled with lines, ideas, rewrites, etc. He labors over his songs as if he were polishing diamonds. Young is more of an inspiration writer, and the songs emerge as if by accident. If you look at the lyrics of these two writers, the differences in style are obvious. Simon's lyrics seem very careful, almost meticulous, while Young's seem more like explosions of energy that take off in many different directions.

Only by writing a number of songs will it become clear to you where you fit into this picture. I have written songs in both ways, and I honestly can't say that one way works better for me than the other. I have even worked on a theatrical project and virtually dreamed a song. I woke up early in the morning and the song seemed to write itself, solving some particular problem in the theatrical action. I've also written songs over fairly long periods of time, where the entire focus of the song changed but I was able to retain a few key lines or concepts.

WORK HABITS

Each writer has to decide on the best way that he or she can work. Some people work best in the morning, with a minimum of distractions. Some work best in a particular room with certain tools spread out around them. These may be a piano, a tape recorder, a synthesizer, a notebook or whatever. Some people work best at night, when the world has come to a stop and they are alone with their thoughts. Others work best in a separate office away from home, where they treat songwriting as a regular job rather than an avocation. In Nashville I have heard some writers talk about "going in to the office." Some people need to be able to make a quick cup of coffee, while others don't want any conceivable kind of distraction to interrupt them. This is not the romantic image that most people would identify with artistry of any kind.

It is up to you to determine what time of day is best and what tools you require. If you reach the creative impasse we call "writer's block," then a change of venue or habits is a useful remedy. The notion here is that you have become bored with your own particular routines, and you require a change in order to be inspired again. For some people it isn't a matter of changing their work habits, but more the idea of traveling to some new place and experiencing something new. I remember reading that John D. Loudermilk, a successful Nashville writer and author of, among other songs, "Tobacco Road," likes to take train trips for inspiration. He finds there is something about the sound of the train and being away from home that inspires him. Other writers work well on airplanes or in automobiles. (We don't recommend strumming the guitar while driving.)

One useful tool to have is a battery-operated tape recorder. You can keep it by your bed, in your car, or wherever you seem to get ideas when using a notebook is out of the question. You should also have some notebooks that you can use to jot down ideas, lines, titles or entire songs.

Cell phones and answering machines can also be used if you are away from home. Simply sing your lyric and tune into the machine.

Currently there are portable digital tape recorders available that also enable you to add additional vocal or instrumental parts.

SONG TYPES

There are many different kinds of songs, and each subject has its own logic. Let's take a look at the song types in terms of subject matter, and then discuss them in terms of musical genres.

BALLADS

In folk songs, a ballad is a song that tells a story. It can be about any number of things—a historical event, a contemporary disaster, a knight's quest in olden times. This form is somewhat rare in contemporary music, but the disaster genre was quite a valid form in the music of the early twentieth century. Occasionally the ballad form is used in contemporary country music, although the genre has essentially been folded into the story song. Events such as earthquakes, tornadoes or mine cave-ins occasionally still inspire this particular genre.

POWER BALLADS

In contemporary pop music a ballad is usually a story about some sort of love affair. Ballads tend to be slow and somewhat melancholy. The power ballad is the ballad shifted into overdrive. Artists like Whitney Houston, Celine Dion and Mariah Carey are fond of power ballads because they retain the subject matter of the pop ballad but generally rise to extreme emotional heights and musical pitches. In this style one writes about deathless love affairs. Tragedy and total bliss are the themes that work, not the casual love affair or the understated romance.

I have always wanted to do a word count of the songs Celine Dion has recorded to see how many of them use the word *love*. I can hardly think of a song that she has recorded that doesn't use the word numerous times. The lyrical key to the power ballad is the use of highly emotional lyrics and the avoidance of understatement. Obviously there is a strong market for songs that express all of the many emotions that go with intimate relationships.

STORY SONGS

Story songs are songs that tell a story. They are usually organized into a beginning, middle and ending, and they don't skip around with tangential thoughts, as many other song forms might do. The focus of the lyric should be on advancing the story line. Anything that gets in the way is irrelevant and should be excised when you do your rewriting. This style of song is common in country music, whether it is a story like the one told in Don Schlitz's "The Gambler" or humorous examples like Jerry Reed's "Tupelo, Mississippi Flash."

Artists who have a folk background are fond of story songs, because of the link they represent to their roots in traditional ballads. Harry Chapin was an absolute master of this form. In the song "Taxi" he talked about the accidental reunion of two former lovers, and how the woman had sold out her acting dreams for a wealthy and secure life, while her lover's dreams of becoming a pilot had degenerated into marijuana-addled trips in his taxicab. Chapin wrote many other story songs, such as "W-O-L-D," the tale of a sad, middle-aged disc jockey whose career is going nowhere but down.

Some other great examples of story songs are Gordon Lightfoot's "Wreck of the Edmund Fitzgerald," about a shipwreck on the Great Lakes, and John McCutcheon's song "Christmas In The Trenches." McCutcheon's song is about a strange incident that occurred in World War I, when German and British soldiers declared an impromptu truce on Christmas Eve, and sang together for one long and peaceful night.

SONG SUBJECTS

It is also possible to look at songs in terms of subject matter as well as style. For example, songs about specific places, countries or climates seem to have a certain fascination for the listener. A song like "By the Time I Get to Phoenix" is a veritable travelogue, carrying with it a variety of rich connotations for the listener. Think of the number of songs that mention cities, states, or countries. Jimmy Webb seems particularly fond of the genre with his "Wichita Lineman" and "Galveston." Add to the list "Georgia on my Mind," "Houston," "Route 66," "Brazil," "Back Home Again in Indiana," "I Left My Heart in San Francisco," "Summer Dreams," "Autumn in New York," "Moonlight in Vermont," "Kansas City" and dozens of others. The old country standard "I'm Movin' On" names city after city in its lyric. The listener expects that a song about, say, Brazil, will be more exotic than one about Houston. Locating a song in a specific place may also immediately tell you what sort of musical style is appropriate to use.

Songs that offer nonspecific but generically religious inspiration such as "You'll Never Walk Alone" also have a broad appeal. Dance songs, which may or may not introduce a new dance, also are atmospheric and well-received by a mass audience. It helps, of course, if the dance catches on. Think of all the songs that accompanied or introduced such dances as the monkey, the samba, the twist, the lambada, etc.

Christmas songs offer popularity for a limited amount of time each year, but the few that really catch on may last for years. "White Christmas" and "The Christmas Song (Chestnuts Roasting on an Open Fire)" are two outstanding examples. My good friend Dan Fox told me recently that he has written thirteen different musical arrangements for various publications featuring "Rudolph the Red-Nosed Reindeer."

In times of national stress, patriotic songs often catch on. They may be associated with wars, heroic deeds, landmark events in history or other important phenomena.

ROMANCE

Love is still the primary subject of popular music. Love songs can be divided into various categories, most of which are fairly obvious. One subject is infatuation— boy loves girl, or girl loves boy. In these songs the loved one is wonderful and can do no wrong. One approach to such songs is the Romeo and Juliet style, where the love must triumph over such obstacles as family opposition. Or the situation may not work out, as in the play, for the same reason. There is also the opposite sort of song, where the lover feels that he has been wronged. In this sort of plot things haven't worked out, and the singer is bitter about it. Dylan's "If I Had It to Do All Over Again, I'd Do It All Over You," and "Don't Think Twice, It's Allright" are examples of this style. There are also songs that detail the failings of one or the other protagonist in the relationship, or both.

Love songs may be idealistic and airy, or they may express the physical relationship in a fairly explicit manner. Certain singers are fond of the dramatic love song genre, which is usually presented in the form of the power ballad. These songs are generally chock-full of similes, metaphors and dramatic situations. They generally require extreme vocal ranges and often have giant melodic leaps, intended to enhance the song's dramatic elements.

Cheating songs are another side of the love song coin. This is a classic genre of country song. Almost invariably it is the man who is cheating. Mac McAnally's "All These

Years," which was a big hit for Sawyer Brown, provided a different look at this genre. In this song the man comes home early and finds the woman in bed with someone else. The two then examine their relationship and realize it is best for them to stay together.

Let's move on to different musical genres, and talk about appropriate lyrics in these styles.

RAP MUSIC LYRICS

All of the negative publicity that rap music receives in the media has masked the clever use of words that can be found in many rap songs. In a sort of Bob Dylan-y way, rap lyrics feature run-on sentences, lines without end and rhyme schemes that pop in and out of the lyrics. Rather than telling a single story, the best rap songs seem to have as many story lines as a sophisticated screenplay. Many words are invented, and the emphasis is on the use of current street slang. For this reason rap songs tend to date themselves, because the particular images that are fresh in a new song become old hat by the time ten artists have mined the same phrases. On the other hand, issues such as police brutality and economic inequity regrettably seem to have a recurrent and lengthy shelf life in the black community.

Another stream of rap music utilizes lyrics where the rapper challenges another artist in the same idiom. These lyrics are sort of the contemporary equivalent of jazz cutting contests, when rival saxophone players, for example, would compete head-to-head for audience approval.

ROCK 'N' ROLL

There are so many genres of rock 'n' roll that it would be easy to write an entire book about writing rock songs. Old-time rock 'n' roll 1950s style is still quite popular, especially in country music. These songs tend to have easygoing and simple lyrics about girls, cars, romance, etc. Heavy metal music tends to indulge in harder-edged, gloom-and-doom scenarios, with lots of drama and crisis situations. Teenage self-pity and the decadence of society are popular subjects.

Alternative rock often features more abstract lyrics. Often the story lines are complex and don't lead in one particular direction. Rhythm and blues and soul-oriented music tend to be grittier and more involved with realistic, everyday dilemmas, like the song "If Loving You Is Wrong, I Don't Want To be Right," recorded by Luther Ingram.

Like it or not, there always seems to be a market for bubblegum music, music for pre-teens. This is the audience cultivated by New Kids on the Block, the Backstreet Boys and Justin Bieber. The lyrics tend to be simple and devoid of any element of risk, whether it's drugs or sex or anything else.

BROADWAY SONGS AND STANDARDS

The word standard indicates that a song has entered the repertoire of a variety of singers and been recorded by many of them. Artists like Tony Bennett and Peggy Lee and younger singers like Michael Feinstein, Barbara Cook and Amanda McBroom are examples of singers who record in this genre. The good news for songwriters is that most of these artists do not write their own songs, so they have to use material by professional songwriters.

In this genre of song the emphasis is on sophistication. The rhymes are almost perfect, the subject matter and story lines are usually clever, and the melodies and harmonic progressions are relatively complex. In the case of songs used in Broadway shows, the primary goal of the song is to advance the action in the show. This can be done by writing songs about characters in the play or situations that reveal emotions that may or may not be present in the book of the show. Usually the lyricist in a Broadway show is a different person than the one who writes the melody, and often a third person writes the book, as the script is called. This is partly because pre-Broadway tryouts often require that new songs be written overnight, rehearsed immediately and then placed in the show in order to test their dramatic efficacy. Two people who work well together can often do this more quickly and efficiently than a solo songwriter is able to do.

MOVIE SONGS

In the past ten years there has been an increasing emphasis on the use of songs in movies. Before that time a movie often had a song at the beginning or the end, but the bulk of the music in films was instrumental. Such movies as *Flashdance* changed the nature of movie scores so that some films consist of what are termed "song scores," collections of songs that are surrounded by only a relatively small amount of instrumental music. Most of these songs are performed by well-known artists, with an increasing emphasis on current hitmakers.

The songs used in movies—when they are not pop songs—tend to be a simplified version of Broadway show music. The songs must be relevant (at least to an extent) to the film, but they aren't necessarily as involved in characterization or plot lines as their Broadway counterparts. Currently we are seeing soundtrack albums that actually feature songs that are not in the film. The songs are used to promote the film, and the film in turn also serves to promote the songs and the soundtrack album.

Other songs may be used in movie trailers, previews that advertise movies. Songs in trailers generally do not appear in the actual movie or in any subsequent soundtrack albums.

CHILDREN'S SONGS

There are a variety of genres of music written for children. The Disney-style song, written by such songwriters as the Sherman brothers or Richard and Marilyn Bergman, are middle-of-the-road songs that are often simplified versions of Broadway show tunes. Folk-oriented artists like Raffi write kids' songs that are modern-day versions of folk songs. Many of them are designed to aid children in developing a positive self-image. They may discuss such matters as the notion of giving kids permission to fail, or helping kids to get along with one another. Kids' songs written and performed by rock 'n' rollers are now starting to appear.

Raffi himself started his career in rock 'n' roll. So did current children's song artist, Dan Zanes, who was in the band the Del Fuegos.

The children's market is a bit peculiar in the sense that you are really writing songs for two people, the children and their parents. It can be a bit tricky to appeal to both groups. In any case the lyrics need to be simple and coherent so that children can easily remember them. Remember that tunes written for younger children to sing need to have simple melodies with a limited vocal range.

LATIN MUSIC

As the percentage of the Spanish-speaking population increases, there is a stronger market for songs written in Spanish, or written in both Spanish and English. There is a strong Cuban population in Florida, a substantial Puerto Rican population on the eastern seaboard, and a huge Mexican-American population throughout the Southwest.

These songs are often both romantic and rhythmic, which may appear contradictory but works in this idiom. If you speak Spanish it may well behoove you to start writing lyrics in both languages.

A large segment of the Mexican-American population has responded to songs about narcotics trafficking. These songs are called *narcocorridos*, and some of the bands recording them, like Los Tigres del Norte, have sold millions of records. Another popular subject involved in this idiom concerns illegal immigrants and border crossings. In my opinion, African-American music has been a dominant influence on American pop music in the twentieth century, and I expect that in the twenty-first century Latin music will have as strong an impact on the pop music scene.

NOVELTY SONGS

Novelty songs are songs about absurd situations. They often utilize nonsense syllables and implausible situations. Country artist Ray Stevens is one of the masters of this genre, and humorist Weird Al Yankovic has added the notion of parodies of existing hits. He transformed "My Sharona" into "My Bologna," and "Beat It" into "Eat It." Keep in mind that if you decide to write parodies it is necessary to get permission from and share the rights with the composer of the original song. Ignoring this can lead to unpleasant lawsuits. Not all composers are amused by parodies of their work.

HOLIDAY AND SPECIAL EVENT SONGS

There is a small but not entirely insignificant market for Christmas songs. The object is to write a song like Mel Torme's "The Christmas Song (Chestnuts Roasting on an Open Fire)," or Irving Berlin's "White Christmas." The sales and airplay on these songs is phenomenal, if seasonal.

There are other songs that are commissioned for special events, such as the 100th birthday of a town, a song commemorating a specific event in a city or state's history, and so on. These songs generally pay a flat fee, although the author can retain his or her rights and, often, the publishing. In order to write songs of this nature the songwriter often has to research the history of a town. Sometimes there are contests for these jobs, and the decision as to whether it is worthwhile to enter the contest is largely dependent upon what the reward will be. Although I am generally unenthusiastic about song "contests," if you have no previous credits it isn't a bad way to build your songwriting résumé. Sometimes further money is available to record or produce the recording of the song.

CONTEMPORARY FOLK SONGS

Although the literal definition of a folk song is that it has passed into tradition and no one knows who the original composer was, there are artists like John Prine, Tom Paxton, Suzanne Vega, the Indigo Girls and Tracy Chapman who write in this vein. The emphasis is on story lines, but they may not be as coherent as in the actual story song form. The subjects of these songs tend to be contemporary concerns, such as the environment or the life of the "common man." When such songs discuss concern romantic situations they tend to be somewhat complex.

A number of these songs, in both the folk and country vein, deal with asserting the rights of women. "Independence Day," a huge country hit written by Gretchen Peters and recorded by Martina McBride, is about spousal abuse, and Suzanne Vega's "Luka" is about child abuse.

One of the aspects of folk songs that Bob Dylan popularized in the early part of his career involves social protest. This can include complaints about governmental actions, lyrics focusing on the denial of rights to the underprivileged, or songs depicting the injustice of racial prejudice.

Billy Bragg and Steve Earle are among a number of song-writers who deal with social issues. John Trudell, a Native American poet and activist, has also found something of an audience with his songs about Indian rights and issues.

COUNTRY MUSIC

As in rock 'n' roll, there are many styles of country music. Traditionalist lyrics tend to deal with the everyday lives of poor or average citizens. The subject of husbands or wives cheating on one another is a style of its own. At the same time other songs tend to celebrate more traditional values, like Earl Thomas Conlee's "The Old School." Other common song topics include drinking and truck driving. Writers like Mary Chapin Carpenter and Nanci Griffith have one foot in country music and the other in folk. They tend to write a rich mixture of songs, some about traditional country subjects and others that are more in the vein of story songs. Bluegrass songs tend to worship the traditional lifestyles, but also include subjects common to other country songs, such as romance.

JAZZ

Many jazz tunes do not utilize lyrics. The ones that do often feature "scat singing," using meaningless syllables for their sound value. The singers in these styles use their voices to simulate the lines that horn players play. The lyrics generally reflect the sort of sophistication found in Broadway tunes and popular music standards.

There is a fundamental difference in the way jazz singers perform, as opposed to pop, rock or country singers. Jazz singers may improvise on the lyrics or melody of a song; they often deliberately sing in front of or behind the beat, and they may take rhythmic liberties with lyrics and melodies. This is comparable to what a jazz horn player might do when performing a pop standard like the song

"Stardust," as opposed to someone who plays the melody without any sort of embellishments.

Norah Jones has become an enormously popular artist and songwriter, writing and/or performing music that contains jazz, pop and even country elements.

GOSPEL MUSIC AND THE CHRISTIAN MARKET

Gospel is divided into white and black music styles. Literally, it is the music that is sung in churches. Both styles of music have come under pressure to cross over by producing songs that achieve popularity in the broad marketplace as well as with the devoutly religious audience. There are even heavy metal and rap Christian artists, who are attempting to reach younger audiences with a religious message.

There is some controversy about such contemporary Christian artists as Amy Grant and Michael W. Smith and their rap and metal counterparts, like Stryper. Sometimes their lyrics tend to combine personal and religious images, and this is offensive to some deeply religious people.

Crossover religious music contains lyrics that peripherally religious people can identify with. Part of the purpose of this music is to convert the audience to a more religious stance. More traditional gospel lyrics are uncompromising and primarily reflect a devout belief in God.

THE INFLUENCE OF BOB DYLAN AND THE BEATLES

Bob Dylan and the Beatles transformed the lyrics of American popular music some thirty-five to forty years ago. Before they began to write songs, the fundamental subjects present in American popular music were romance and novelty lyrics. There was an almost complete absence of lyrics that reflected the lives of the average person.

Dylan also pioneered the use of abstract lyrics with sentences of indefinite length. The Beatles helped solidify Dylan's position by writing songs about any subject under the sun. It also became obligatory for pop artists to write their own songs. This situation continues today, outside the mold of country music. In country music there are still numerous songwriters who make a living writing songs for other people and who do not regard themselves as performers.

Before the Beatles and Dylan started to write their songs, references to popular music in novels or in college classes almost invariably dealt with jazz. As Dylan and the Beatles became popular, it seemed that American popular music had grown up and had become relevant to the lives of intelligent people. This is not to deny the cleverness and craft of such writers as Rodgers and Hart or Cole Porter. That is a different subject.

If you want to study how lyrics evolved, buy some songbooks that contain Dylan's and Lennon and McCartney's songs. It would be difficult to find better teachers.

SONGS AND THE ARTIST'S IMAGE

Several books about songwriting assert that it isn't a good idea to write songs that make the artist look bad to her audience. Although this is certainly true for some artists, there are a number of autobiographical songs that artists have written about themselves that portray the artist in a negative light. Robert Cray's "Strong Persuader" portrays him as a cad, making love to his best friend's wife just

for the hell of it, although he is well aware of the consequences. On Joni Mitchell's first album she described herself as "a cactus tree, so busy being free." This is hardly a positive way to look at oneself.

Of course these are autobiographical songs, written by the artist. Nevertheless I tend to avoid generalizing about what sort of songs constitute "forbidden territory." It all depends on the audience you are striving to reach.

GENERALIZATIONS AND RULES

In general, given the broad range of songs and song subjects that have been introduced to popular music ever since Dylan and the Beatles became hit writers, I tend to shy away from philosophizing about what works and what doesn't work in pop songs. There is no question that a knowledge of "the rules" is going to help you define what is going to work for you in your writing career. But beware of assumptions of what will and what won't work. My point of view is that the writer has to strike a balance between what he or she is comfortable with and what the commercial world of music publishing or record companies will accept. Remember that the Beatles were turned down by every record company in England—twice. Likewise, virtually every songwriter and artist can list dozens of rejections they experienced before they achieved any sort of success.

At the same time I have attended countless music business seminars where the artist and repertoire (A&R) representatives of record companies have piously discoursed that artists and writers should be original and never copy anyone. The truth is that anything that is truly new and original usually has a hard time being accepted by major record companies. Their willingness to take risks is, to put it mildly, limited.

CHAPTER 4 RESOURCES

The Braheny, Blume and Citron books listed as resources for Chapter 3 are also useful here. Both Braheny and Blume claim that it is a mistake to write songs that portray artists in a negative light. In my opinion, this is not always an accurate statement.

In the book *Solo: Women Singer-Songwriters In Their Own Words*, edited by Marc Woodworth, published by Delta Books in 1998. The interview with Joan Osborne on pages 183-198 describes her use of webbing. The same technique is used in public schools to brainstorm various creative processes.

In Braheny's book, and Sheila Davis' *The Songwriter's Idea Book*, published by Writer's Digest Books in 1992, there is a considerable amount of discussion of left brain/right brain theory and creativity. They also describe other exercises designed to expand your creativity as a writer.

Rhymes, Titles and Hooks

Most of the existing books on songwriting are straightforward in asserting the differences between songs and poems, and yet when they start to explain lyric writing they deal with rhyme schemes in the same way that poetry books do. They talk about masculine and feminine rhymes, iambic pentameter meters and so forth. Some of this sort of material will appear in the appendix of this book, but in the main body of the text I am going to take a more down-to-earth approach.

The other aspect of rhymes and form that is confusing is that many singers do not sing a song in the way that someone might read the lyric who has not heard the melody. I have already mentioned that many singers extend and contract the length of lines at will. They also add syllables like "ooh-ooh," or "whoa," or "yay, yay," or as in Frank Sinatra's version of "Strangers in the Night," "dooby, dooby do."

This means that the carefully crafted lines and rhymes have been totally revised according to the singer's inspiration, convenience or stubbornness (you choose which is most applicable). The songwriter often plays no role in this process; it's more of a decision made by the singer or the record producer, or a spur-of-the-moment improvisation

that happens at the studio, suggested by the drummer, the background singer or a member of the singer's entourage.

RHYMES

First of all, not all songs rhyme. Many songs that rhyme do not use a single consistent rhyme scheme. They may rhyme lines internally, use rhymes in parts of the song and not in others, or use the sort of run-on sentences that are typical of Dylan's early songs, with rhyme after rhyme throughout.

The advantage of rhymes is simply that they make songs easier to remember, and they provide material that makes the singer's work easier. If we take a lyric that contains four lines for each verse, the obvious place for the rhymes to occur is at the end of the lines. Theoretically the songwriter could make lines 1 and 3, or 2 and 4 rhyme, or 1 and 2, or 3 and 4, or 1 and 4 and 2 and 3. It is also not necessary to use the same rhyme scheme for the verse and the chorus of a song, nor is it necessary for all parts of the song to rhyme. On the following page is a verse and a chorus of a song I wrote called "Blind Gary," which can be found on the CD that accompanies this book.

2 "Blind Gary"

VERSE

I just got into town,
I was barely seventeen years old;
It was in New York City,
And the East Side winds blew cold.
As I climbed up the stairs,
I heard the sounds of a blues guitar,

CHORUS

And Blind Gary played the blues for you,
Blind Gary played the blues for me,
Blind Gary played the blues for a song,
As though it were the very last time.

Notice that lines 2 and 4 of the verse rhyme. The fifth and sixth lines of the song act as a pre-hook, and neither they nor the chorus rhyme. However, the chorus has the repeated words "Blind Gary played." This sets up a sort of chant, which in effect substitutes for rhyme.

The song below, "The Eye That Never Sleeps," was written for the aforementioned play about Jesse James and his gang, and is intended to be light and humorous.

3 "The Eye That Never Sleeps"

VERSE

There's a band of desperate men,
Do anything to harm you.
They'll rob you on the banks or trains,
They'll try hard to alarm you.

CHORUS

Then call for Pinkerton's mighty men,
A trust we're pledged to keep,
We'll do our best to save the West,
The eye that never sleeps, never sleeps.

Notice that the rhymes occur internally, or inside the lines. The words *harm* in line 2 of the verse and *alarm* in line 4 rhyme, but the ends of the verse lines do not rhyme. In the chorus there is an internal rhyme in line 3 with the words *best* and *West*, and line 4 repeats the phrase "never sleeps," again substituting for a rhyme.

Rhymes can come at the ends of lines, within the lines themselves or not at all. Rhymes can also be imperfect, with words like *finger* and *ginger*, as opposed to, say, *finger* and *linger*. Rhymes can be made with simple one-syllable words like *joy* and *coy* or with two-syllable words like *ranger* and *danger*. It is also possible to rhyme words with three or more syllables.

POSITIVE AND NEGATIVE ASPECTS OF RHYME, AND USING RHYMING TOOLS

Many writers use resources like rhyming dictionaries or thesauruses when they get stuck for rhymes. Obviously the writer should use anything that proves to be helpful. The problem with using these tools is twofold: First of all, you often end up with a list of clumsy words or syllables that is more distracting than it is useful. In the second place, going to a rhyming dictionary may remove you from the process of actually completing a song, and may be more of an impediment than a help. What is going to work for you is very much a function of your own songwriting process. If you are the sort of writer who labors over lyrics, then these tools probably will not keep you from completing a song. If you are more of an "inspiration" writer, someone who works very quickly, it is probably better to use the tools after you establish the basic outline of the song.

The same generalizations apply to the use of rhymes. If your song ideas are being forced into rhyming patterns that aren't especially inventive or interesting, then you may want to be more flexible about using rhymes, and even try to abandon them. The fact is, however, that most commercial songs do rhyme.

TITLES AND HOOKS

A catchy title is a very important element in getting people to remember *your* song rather than the dozens of others that they may hear in a particular day. "I Love You Very Much" isn't a good choice because there are probably a thousand songs copyrighted under that title. It is not possible, by the way, to copyright a title and prevent other people from using it. However, I don't suggest that you write a song and call it "Eleanor Rigby." Certain songs are so identified with their titles that your song will be ignored simply because of the title you have chosen.

Unusual titles can serve to get the listener's (or the music publisher's) attention. Usually the title appears in the chorus or at the beginning or end of the verse, or both. A hook, as mentioned earlier, is a recurrent phrase, musical or lyrical, that is repeated in a song, often numerous times. A catchy guitar part or chorus lyric will enable the listener to remember the song title and sing along with a record on the radio. Introductions to songs serve as hooks, even though they may not be part of the song's originally composed structure. It may be the guitar player on the session or the music arranger who has come up with the part. When a song title is different from the central hook of the song, it tends to confuse the public. This doesn't guarantee that a song won't be successful, but it can be an impediment to success. In the 1980s I played on a number of occasions in Casper and Cheyenne, Wyoming, in a band that did no original music, only cover songs written and performed by others. People invariably asked us to do John Fogerty's song "Proud Mary."

Since the words *Proud Mary* are not the central hook of the song, invariably they would ask for the song they thought was called "Rollin' on the River." For a beginning songwriter it is probably a good idea *not* to use a title that is peripheral to the song's plot and that's rarely mentioned in the song.

Not everyone writes straightforward pop songs, and so when someone like Bob Dylan writes a song with the title "Positively Fourth Street" it works in the overall context of what this particular artist is doing. Even Dylan, however, had his biggest hits with relatively straightforward, hook-titled songs such as "Like a Rolling Stone," "Knockin' on Heaven's Door," and "Lay, Lady Lay."

The third section of this book discusses various musical styles, and what happens when you put lyrics and melodies together. You should now be ready to take a look at writing melodies.

CHAPTER 5 RESOURCES

Add to the Braheny, Blume and Citron books Jimmy Webb's *Tunesmith: Inside the Art of Songwriting*, New York, Hyperion Press, 1998.

Melodic Invention

TYPES OF MELODIES

At the risk of oversimplifying, I would say that there are two kinds of melodies in American popular music. The first has a limited vocal range, and is designed so that the listener can sing along or learn the song without much difficulty. The second sort of melody is designed to show off the technical abilities of a singer. It has a wide vocal range, beyond what the average person could execute. Singers like Celine Dion, Whitney Houston or Mariah Carey generally perform the second style of song. Often these songs involve virtuoso displays of vocal talent, with wide leaps up or down that the average person might have trouble even hearing, let alone executing.

A variation on the complex melodic school of songwriting is the kind of song that doesn't necessarily require a tremendous range on the part of the singer but is nonetheless difficult to execute. This may be because the song is rhythmically complex, because the notes of the melody don't necessarily follow one another easily, or because the writer has created difficult changes in the key or tempo.

If you are writing songs that are not specifically designed for a singer with considerable vocal talent, it is wise to attempt to write melodies that most singers can readily execute. This means that the melodies should:

1) Not have a large number of notes (and words) that make the lyric and melody hard to follow.

2) Be in a normal vocal range. If the song has a vocal range of much more than an octave (C to C one octave higher, for example), it may be difficult for some singers to execute.

3) Have a rhythm that fits comfortably with the song's lyric and general concept (ie., it is probably inappropriate to write a beautiful melody to a song about violence, unless you are deliberately doing it to be ironic. This might work in a Broadway show, but is less likely to be acceptable in a pop song).

4) Avoid enormous vocal leaps that a normal singer can't execute.

5) Be enjoyable for you and others to sing .

If you are writing for a particular artist, the song should be in a musical vein that the artist finds comfortable. Often the best melodies feel almost familiar to the listener, even though they are original so that the listener doesn't think they are borrowed from existing tunes.

WHERE DO MELODIES COME FROM?

There is no set rule about the way melodies are born. Songwriters and composers use a number of techniques. Eventually you will figure out what method works best for you. At that point you will probably stick to that technique, until such time as you feel that your melodies are becoming repetitious or boring. Below are descriptions of the various ways people write melodies, with some discussion of the positive and negative aspects of each style.

WRITING IN YOUR HEAD, AWAY FROM AN INSTRUMENT

Children often spontaneously make up melodies while they are riding in a car, playing or even watching television. Traditionally, classical composers had the attitude that a composer should be capable of hearing melodies in his head and then writing them down. Composers who worked at the piano were thought to be using the instrument as a crutch because they hadn't fully developed their craft. When twentieth-century composer Igor Stravinsky revealed that he worked at the piano, some other composers also admitted that they worked with the piano as well.

The advantage of writing melodies in your head is that you are not limited by the extent of your instrumental skills. Ther are also some melodies that might not be appropriate for the particular instrument that you play. The disadvantage is that you may not be an especially good singer, so that the melodies you write may not sound good to you. This can be quite discouraging. On the other hand, if you are a good guitarist, picking out a melody on the guitar may sound fine.

WRITING WITH A MUSICAL INSTRUMENT

Generally, songwriters favor either the piano or the guitar. Both instruments are capable of playing chords as well as melody lines, although it is probably easier to play them simultaneously on the piano. It is also simple to pick out melodies on the piano. Of course guitarists can do this as well, but the notes on the guitar don't sustain as long, and it takes a somewhat higher skill level to pick melody notes on it than on a keyboard instrument. Guitar is such a chordal instrument that songwriters who play guitar often fall into the trap of creating melodies that are derived directly from chord progressions, rather than standing out as melodies in their own right. On the other hand, the guitar is portable, and you can write with it in the desert, at a mountain lake or at a friend's house.

Reasonably capable guitarists can come up with interesting strumming patterns that can really bring a song to life. This is a bit more difficult to do on a keyboard instrument.

The question of whether writing with a musical instrument is advantageous is often dependent on the extent of the songwriter's instrumental skills. If you are always having to search to find the right chord, or if you are unable to reproduce what you hear in your head on an instrument, then playing while writing is probably an impediment to your particular creative process.

On the other hand, if playing comes easily to you, the guitar or the piano may very well lead you in musical directions that you would never have discovered just by humming or singing a song to yourself. It is also quite common for good songwriters to be adept at coming up with simple yet catchy fills on the guitar or piano. These melodic or rhythmic fragments set the tone for songs, and often end up being used when the song is recorded by artists. Studio musicians might come up with more elaborate or complex musical ideas, but many songwriters seem to have an instinct for developing musical figures that work perfectly with their songs.

Even if you are adept at playing, you need to consider the

idea that most of your instrumental prowess may be in a specific style, or a few specific styles of music. Will this limit the range of melodic ideas that you come up with, and consequently be a barrier in exploring different musical genres?

Songwriters who tend to write while playing an instrument often own several guitars or keyboards, in order to get the inspiration that different sound textures can provide. A twelve-string guitar, for example, sounds quite different than a six-string guitar. It can be an excellent choice for writing a melody that demands a powerful rhythmic impetus in its accompaniment.

My own experience is that when I play a new guitar at a music store, a really interesting guitar seems to inspire me to play a rhythm pattern or a melodic fragment that seems to have come out of the air. Over the years I have probably bought too many instruments that stimulated my creative juices in this way.

CHORD PROGRESSIONS

Chord progressions are simply combinations of chords. There may be only two chords in an entire song, though three-chord songs are much more common. On rare occasions a song may have a single chord, and will basically consist of a simple but catchy rhythmic groove.

Songwriters have different attitudes about writing from chord progressions. Jimmy Webb and Brian Wilson, certainly two of the most creative songwriters of the last half of the 20th century, frankly acknowledge that they sit down at the piano and try out different chord progressions. conversely, successful songwriter Jason Blume strongly recommends that you not do this.

My own feeling is that there isn't a correct approach here. If you have a very limited knowledge of chords on the guitar and the piano, then certainly working with the few chords that you know is not apt to produce outstanding results. On the other hand, knowing a lot about harmony doesn't mean you should use all your knowledge all the time. If you are one of those people who place several dozen chords in their songs, it can be an impediment to writing graceful, flowing melodies.

If you write songs that use complex chord progressions, it may be difficult for other people to learn them quickly. This can inhibit other artists from; recording your songs. If you are only concerned with your own recordings of your songs, this is unimportant.

If you do have a good working knowledge of harmony, writing from chord progressions may be a worthwhile way for you to work. Sometimes writers use dense chord formations that contain a great deal of motion to disguise the fact that the melody itself is undistinguished. In other words, the decorations exceed the quality of the actual fabric. The result is that people may be impressed with the orchestration, but they won't remember the melody it was supposed to highlight.

Quite a few songs that were written on the guitar, like Neil Young's "Helpless," clearly started out with guitar strums. The melody follows the top note of the guitar chord. Once again, whether this is a workable solution depends on whether you are creative enough in adding extra notes to the chords to make the melodies flow.

RHYTHMS

Heavily emphasized rhythms and grooves are a key part of many forms of dance music, and are also found in rap music and the music of many foreign countries, such as Cuba. In this sort of melody writing the tune actually evolves out of the rhythm that the bass and/or drums set up. As we will see when we discuss the making of demos, it is possible to lock in rhythms and grooves through the use of drum machines and sequencing, even if you don't have a particularly keen sense of rhythm.

WHAT IS A MELODY, AND HOW CAN YOU WRITE ONE?

Take the simplest melody that you know. Be sure to select one that you know the words to. It could be something like "On Top of Old Smoky" or "Oh Susannah." Keep the words intact and rewrite the tune. Change it to anything you please. Don't feel any obligation to keep any part of the melody intact.

◆⑤ "On Top of Old Smoky"

"Old Smoky" is a waltz, in $\frac{3}{4}$ time, which means there are three beats, each of them a quarter note long in each bar of music. It starts on the third beat, so that you would count it as follows:

```
 3   1    2  3  123 123 12 3  1   2    3     123   123 12
On top of old Smoky, all covered with snow
3 1 2   3    123 123 12 3    1    2    3    123  123 12
I lost my true lover,  from courting too slow.
```

There are no rules here, so don't feel obligated to keep the song in waltz time. For that matter don't hesitate to change the style of the song. Imagine it, for example, as a blues. Try it like this:

```
(play chord)      12   34 123      4     1234   12
   On top of old Smoky, all covered with snow
    3    4    1234 12   3     4    1234   12
I lost my true lover, from courting too slow.
```

Listen to the two versions on the CD.

OTHER WAYS OF INVENTING MELODIES

Try the musical equivalent of webbing. Take a specific locale, and write a melody that represents that locale. A melody that is intended to make the listener think of Kentucky is obviously going to sound different from a melody that is supposed to convey the Amazon River and primitive tribes. Get a cassette recorder and record fragments. You may want to use the webbing technique to start your song by coming up with words or concepts that will convey the place you are writing about. I am not talking about lyrics, that's a task for another day.

Let's go back to the Kentucky idea. Here's what your webbing might produce.

Mountains, mining. Bluegrass.

◆④ "Kentucky"
- Poor but honest people. Life "on the margin," difficult to make a living farming or mining.
- Mountain music sound—"high lonesome sound."
- "White man's blues."
- Mostly rural. Small towns.

All of the things ought to convey something that should trigger melodies for you. Rather than actually printing the melody here, listen to the CD and see what we came up with for "Kentucky."

Let's go back to the country song ◆⑥ "The Coffee That You Made for Me Is Grounds for Divorce." First of all, let's decide on a rhythm that will be used in the verse. I am going to draw a line over each word where we will play a chord.

On the day that I first met you, I was barely twenty-two.

It immediately occurs to me that we don't need the word "On." So the line changes to:

/ / // / / / // / / / / / // / / /
The day that I first met you, I was barely twenty-two.

/ / / / // / / // / / // / / /
You said you really liked the things I told you I would do.

/ / / / / / / / / / // / / /
We spent the early mornings at the Crocodile Café

/ / / / / / / / / / / / / / / / /
Drinking lots of java at the start of every day.

Try to imagine what this rhythm will sound like when someone sings it. It is quite "square," meaning that it is sort of stiff and feels like the rhythm that a metronome or a drum machine would play. Let's fool around with the rhythm of the first line a bit:

/ / / / / / / /
The day that I first met you, I was barely twenty-two.

With the rhythm phrased this way the tune sounds more like a folk rock tune, which is not really appropriate for the lyric. We could also do the rhythm in 3/4 time, or waltz time:

/ /
The day that I first met you, I was barely twenty-two.

This is manageable, but a bit awkward.

It seems wise to return to the first version and to do the rest of the song with this pattern. Following is the complete melody, written out in music notation and guitar tablature. You do not need to know how to read music to follow the guitar tablature. Simply put your fingers where the piano notes are indicated; if you are reading the guitar tablature it will tell you what string and fret to play.

◆ 6 "The Coffee That You Made for Me Is Grounds for Divorce"

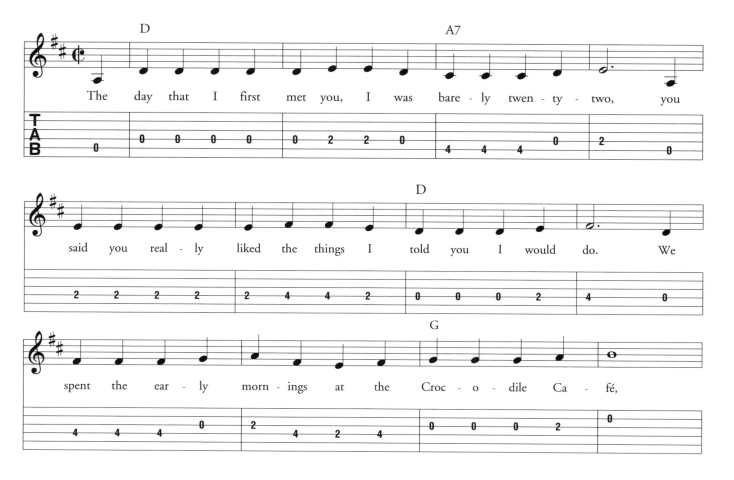

"The Coffee That You Made For Me Is Grounds For Divorce"

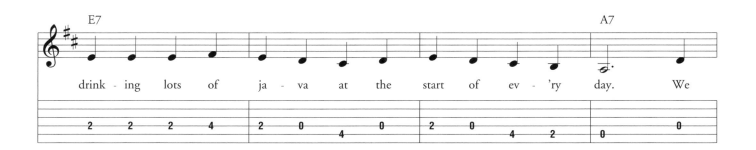

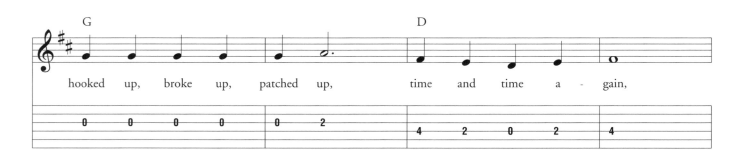

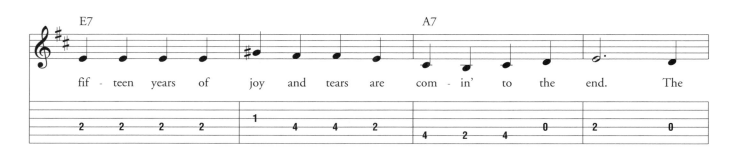

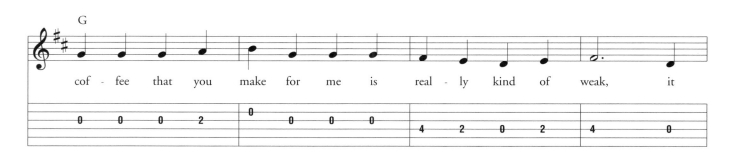

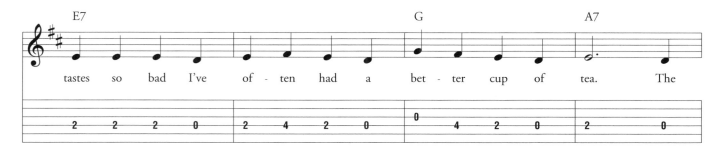

"The Coffee That You Made for Me Is Grounds for Divorce"

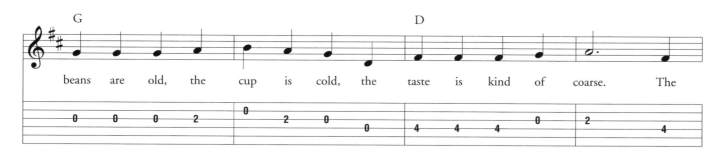

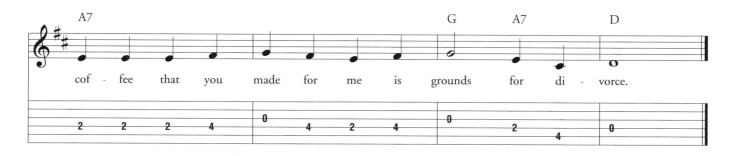

THE DIFFERENCE BETWEEN A MELODY AND AN ARRANGEMENT

What is written above is the melody of the song, with chord symbols indicating the appropriate chords that go with the melody. Musical arrangements are the way that the song gets treated, in terms of the various instruments, tempo or background vocals that are added to the melody. Arrangers are musicians who understand the ways that different instruments work, and how they can add spice to a particular melody. This can be done through the use of musical notation by schooled musicians, or it can evolve through what are known as "head arrangements." A head arrangement occurs when musicians get together and work out different parts of a song while they are learning it. Many popular music recording sessions evolve in this way. Session players are expected to have the skills to add parts to a song that are interesting and appropriate. The same thing happens in rock bands when someone brings in a new song, and the various musicians figure out parts

that add color and life to the melody. In the hands of fine session musicians, the original song is simply the skeleton around which a whole new structure is developed.

Let's go back to the Curtis Mayfield tribute song, "Risin' Above." Take a look at the lyric, and imagine someone singing in a light falsetto. In this song the melody has to have a more fluid shape so that the singer can actually play with the melody and find a rhythmic pattern that will be fluid and flexible.

/   / / / / / / / /   / /
Once upon a time, a man was living in Chicago,

/   / / /   /   /   /   /
Sending out a message to a world he grew to know.

/   /   / /
And the people, they were waiting,

/   /   /   /
For wise words he might tell them,

/ / / / / /   / / /
Some started in to dancing, hoping he would stay.

"Risin' Above"

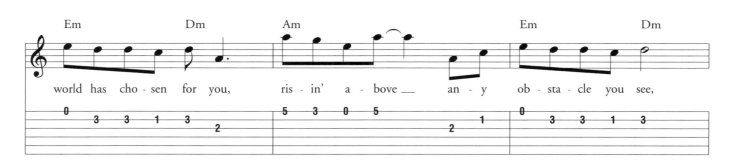

"Risin' Above"

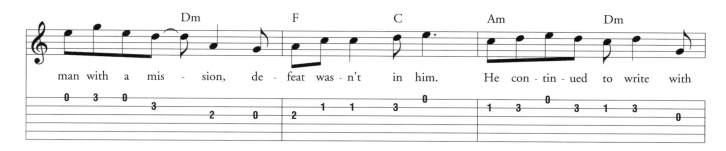

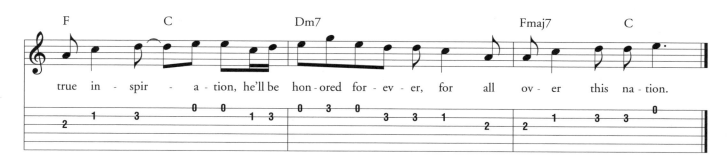

Notice I added the word *out* to the second line so that the melody would be more graceful. In line 4, I changed "to hear what he had to say" to "for wise words he might tell them." I wanted the alliteration of "wise words" with their two w's, and I also felt that the phrase "wise words" was more interesting.

Moving on to the chorus:

```
  /   / /     /     /   / /   /
Risin' above what the world has chosen for you,

 /   / /   /     / / /
Risin' above any obstacle you see,

 /   / / /     /   / /   /   /
Risin' above any harm that's meant to hurt you,

   /     / / /       / / /
Surrounded by love, you can rise above.
```

I changed the chorus lyric in line three from "risin' above, any harm that's meant for you" to "risin' above, any harm that's meant to hurt you," because it seemed to better lend itself to a melody.

```
 /     / / /     /   /     /     /
Then the tragedy struck him, it couldn't defeat him,

   /   / / /     / / /   /
He was a man with a mission, defeat wasn't in him.

 /       / / /   / /   /   /
He continued to write with true inspiration,

   /       / / /     / /
He'll be honored forever, all over this nation.
```

In the bridge I changed the word *so* in line 3 and added the word *true* before *inspiration*. All of these little changes evolve as the words become married to a melody. Sometimes the words have to bend to fit a graceful melodic form, and sometimes the music bends to fit an especially colorful lyric. Since we started with a complete lyric, it is the lyric that changed in this particular example.

On the preceding pages is the complete song, printed in music notation, piano diagrams and guitar tablature.

HOW THE MELODY RELATES TO SONG FORM

In general, people seem to focus on and remember the melodies of choruses. The verses tell the story of a song, but the chorus is the center of attention. Just as the lyric of the chorus needs to be the most powerful part of the song, the melody also needs to stand out over the verses and/or the bridge of a song.

I am referring to the majority of songs, keeping in mind that in some songs the melody is the same or almost identical for the verse and the chorus. We have already seen that in traditional ballads and in children's songs, there may only be an A part to the entire song. There may be no chorus at all.

So the question boils down to how we can make the chorus stand out. The simplest and most obvious way is that the chorus melody is written higher than the verse melody. The problem is that we are far from being the only ones to have figured this out. So it isn't simply a question of singing higher, it's also the problem of coming up with a more interesting chorus melody, or at least one that is more singable and memorable to the listener.

When you finish the song, ask yourself if it is easy for you to remember the chorus. If even the writer finds little difference between a verse melody and a chorus melody, then it's time to go back and rework the chorus.

Because of the chorus's importance, there are some writers who actually start the song by writing a chorus, and then move backward to the verses. You should also give some consideration to reworking the order of verses, substituting one for another, and abandoning verses that don't seem to help the flow of the song.

Finally, let's look at the melody of the bridge. The bridge is generally placed in the song to provide some sort of new melodic and lyric interest. It may represent a new point of view, it may contradict a point of view that the rest of the song expresses, it may really be nothing but a rather elaborate vamp, or it may be so well executed that the writer repeats it more than once in a song. This last option is somewhat unusual, but not unknown. The longer the song, the more apt the writer is to repeat the bridge.

In any case try writing a bridge that contains:
1) A different set of chords than are found in the rest of the song;
2) A melody that is in a different vocal range, whether higher or lower, than the rest of the song.

Generally the bridge returns to the chorus rather than a new verse. Be sure that whatever melody you have written can return to the chorus gracefully.

◆ 7 "THE C MAJOR SCALE"

Try playing the C major scale, diagramed below. The notes are

I II III IV V VI VII VIII (or I of the next ascending scale).
C D E F G A B C

Below are the diagrams for this scale on the guitar and the piano. You can also hear this scale played on the CD that comes with this book.

C Scale

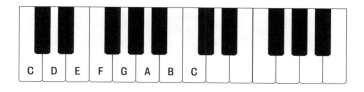

If you look at the diagram, you will see that there are black keys between all of the white keys, except in two places. They are the distances between notes B and C, and E and F. If you are playing the guitar, B is the open second string, and C is the second string fingered at the first fret. E is the open first or the open sixth string, and F is the sixth or first string fingered at the first fret. The other notes on the guitar, for example the distances between C and D, or G and A, are two frets part.

You can build any major scale by placing the notes a whole step (or two frets) apart, except for the distances between the third and fourth and seventh and eighth notes of the scale. It is important to understand the concept of scales, because they form the basis for the melody and the chords in any given song.

OTHER MELODY-WRITING DEVICES

There are a number of other devices that can be utilized in writing melodies. It is possible to take a melodic figure and simply use the same figure with higher pitches. A very simple example is the children's tune "Three Blind Mice." The first phrase "three blind mice," is repeated, and the second phrase, "see how they run," is the same phrase a minor third higher (in the key of C the notes are EDC, EDC, and then G, F, E).

This can also be done by playing the same phrase in a new key. In musical arranging, similar effects are achieved by simply changing the rhythm of the notes. Imagine the same song in a sort of jazz version by making the notes uneven.

CHORDS

As we discussed above, chords are derived from the notes of the scale. Remember the C scale contains the notes

I II III IV V VI VII I of the next octave or VIII.
C D E F G A B C

The C major chord contains the first, third and fifth notes of the scale (CEG.) A C minor chord uses the same notes, except that the E becomes an E♭ (see the diagrams below). Later we will discuss more advanced chords, many of which contain as many as four or five notes.

CHORD PROGRESSIONS AND MELODIES

Some chord progressions are extremely simple to play on the piano and guitar. Try playing the following chord progressions, as found in the piano and guitar diagrams. See if any melodies emerge from these chord sequences. You can also hear these chords on the accompanying CD.

◆ ⑧ PROGRESSION #1: I and V7

There are a handful of songs that utilize only two chords. They are primarily children's songs or folk songs. In the key of C these chords are C and G7, as diagrammed below. The C chord is I in the key of C, and the G7 chord is V because it is based on the fifth note of the C scale.

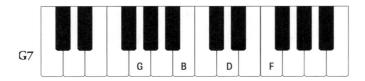

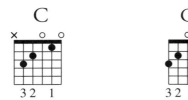

Examples of these two chord songs include "Tom Dooley" and "On Top of Old Smoky."

◆ ⑨ CHORD PROGRESSION #2: I and VI minor C and Am

The roman numeral I refers to the fact that in the key of C, C is the I chord. The notes found in the C chord are CEG. VI minor is the minor chord that is found on the sixth note of the C scale. The notes in this chord are A, C and E. (See the diagrams below.)

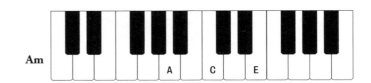

Not many songs utilize these two chords alone, but by adding the Dm7 chord (DFAC) and the G7 chord, (GBDF), you have the chord progression C Am Dm7 G7 and C. This is the chord progression that is utilized in so many '50s rock songs and earlier pop standards. Songs such as "Heart and Soul," "Blue Moon," and "All I Have to Do Is Dream," come to mind.

There are numerous chord progressions found in popular songs; a number of them can be found in the appendix of this book. For now let's turn to a discussion of various musical styles, and how songs are written that clearly fit into these styles.

CHAPTER 6 RESOURCES

There are any number of books available on music theory. I suggest that you NOT turn to them at this time, but proceed to Chapter 7, and the discussion of musical styles. The following two books are almost encyclopedic in nature. You can use them for reference from time to time without having to read through each one quickly.

Rikki Rooksby. *How To Write Songs on Guitar*. Milwaukee, Hal Leonard Books, 2007.

Rikki Rooksby. *How To Write Songs on Keyboards*. Milwaukee, Hal Leonard Books, 2005.

Musical Styles and Songwriting

THE BLUES

Let's start by discussing the blues. Blues melodies have certain specific characteristics that clearly distinguish them from other kinds of tunes. You will remember that we talked about the C scale:

I   II   III IV   V   VI VII VIII (or I of the next octave).
C D E F G A B C

In blues songs the third and seventh notes of the scale are usually lowered by a half step. In other words, the E becomes an E♭, and the B becomes a B♭. So the blues scale is:

C D E♭ F G A B♭ C

⑩ "C BLUES SCALE"

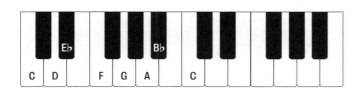

| C   D   E♭   F   G   A   B♭   C |

On the guitar the string is often bent or pulled to one side, so that the E♭ is not really an E♭ but a pitch that is between an E♭ and an E. Similarly the B♭ is between a B♭ and a B note.

Because it isn't possible to bend pitches on a piano (although with pitch bend it can be done on a synthesizer), it is common to play the E♭ and the E notes consecutively. The same thing applies to the B♭ and B notes of the scale. This tends to create the same feeling as you get in pulling the guitar string, although it is not quite as striking a sound.

Good blues singers do the same thing vocally, floating between the note and the flatted note just below it. If you overdo this effect the result can be stiff and grotesque, and takes away from the spontaneity of the blues. Let's try to write a blues melody, and then we can discuss how chords in the blues work.

⑪ "Lookin' for My Baby Blues"

I haven't written the melody in piano tablature, because it would be too complicated. If you are a piano player and can't read music, listen to the CD.

◆ "Lookin' for My Baby Blues"

"Lookin' for My Baby Blues"

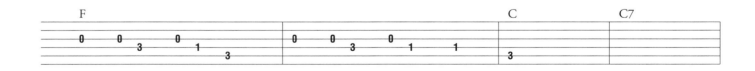

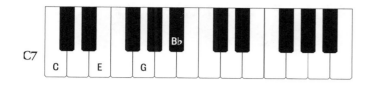

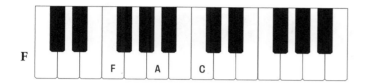

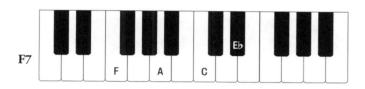

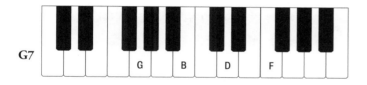

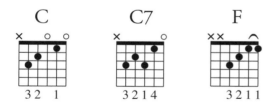

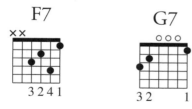

Notice that the major and seventh chords are virtually interchangeable. This is because the seventh chords give you the "blue notes" that we discussed earlier. Remember the blue notes are the third and seventh notes of the chords. For the C chord these notes are E♭ and B♭, and for the F chord they are A♭ and E♭.

DETERMINING KEYS AND CHANGING THEM

It is not unusual for musicians to write songs in keys that are not the best ones for them (or others) to sing in. First of all, let's discuss how you determine the key of a song.

The first way is to look at the key signature. On the left-hand side of the musical staff is a G clef, and next to it there are either sharps, flats or no accidentals at all. (Accidentals is a fancy word for sharps and flats.) Each key signature can represent one of two keys, a major key or its relative minor. The relative minor is three half steps, or three frets, below the major key. The diagrams below will show the key signature for C or A minor. Following the chart below, you will be able to tell what key a song is in. We will then discuss how you can transpose this key, if it proves unsuitable for singing.

KEY IDENTIFICATION CHART

NUMBER OF SHARPS	MAJOR KEY	RELATIVE MINOR KEY
0	C	A minor
1	G	E minor
2	D	B minor
3	A	F♯ minor
4	E	C♯ minor
5	B	G♯ minor
6	F♯	D♯ minor
7	C♯	A♯ minor

NUMBER OF FLATS	MAJOR KEY	RELATIVE MINOR KEY
1	F	D minor
2	B♭	G minor
3	E♭	C minor
4	A♭	F minor
5	D♭	B♭ minor
6	G♭	E♭ minor
7	C♭	A♭ minor

Don't be too concerned about keys that have six or seven flats or sharps. It is rare to see them in popular songs, although it isn't unknown.

Let's go back to our blues song. Let's say that you've decided that the key is just a little too low for you. You'd prefer to sing it in the key of D.

Go back to the diagram. You will notice that if you look at the key of C and D, the D chord will correspond to C when you change from the key of C to D. The G chord or G7 will correspond to the F or F7 chord in the key of C. And the A7 chord in the key of D will correspond to the G7 chord in the key of C. The chords to the song will now be:

 D (formerly C)   D7 (formerly C7)

 Goin' to the river, walkin up and down

  G7 (formerly F7)   D (formerly C) D7 (formerly C7)

Goin' to the river, walkin' up and down

  A7 (formerly A7)

Lookin' for my baby,

  G (formerly F) D G D A7 (formerly C, F, C, G7)

 she just can't be found.

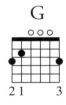
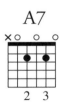

You should be able to hear the difference in the melody in the key quite easily, but if you want to you can perform the same exercise with the melody, and transpose each note in music or tablature to the new key. The same exercise applies when you want to lower the key. In the key of A this song would contain the chords A, A7, D, D7 and E7. Below is a chart of major scales that will enable you to transpose any melody from one key to another.

KEYS WITH SHARPS OR FLATS

SCALE

	I	II	III	IV	V	VI	VII	I
C	C	D	E	F	G	A	B	C
D♭	D♭	E♭	F	G♭	A♭	B♭	C	D♭
D	D	E	F♯	G	A	B	C♯	D
E♭	E♭	F	G	A♭	B♭	C	D	E♭
E	E	F♯	G♯	A	B	C♯	D♯	E
F	F	G	A	B♭	C	D	E	F
G♭	G♭	A♭	B♭	C♭	D♭	E♭	F	G♭
G	G	A	B	C	D	E	F♯	G
A♭	A♭	B♭	C	D♭	E♭	F	G	A♭
A	A	B	C♯	D	E	F♯	G♯	A
B♭	B♭	C	D	E♭	F	G	A	B♭
B	B	C♯	D♯	E	F♯	G♯	A♯	B

(Note: The key of C has no sharps or flats)

Be aware of the fact that C♯ and D♭ are the same pitches, as are D♯ and E♭, F♯ and G♭, G♯ and A♭ and A♯ and B♭. I have omitted the keys of F♯ and C♯, and G♭ and C♭, because they are relatively rare, and they contain so many sharps or flats that the musical spelling leads to such notes as B♯, which is the same pitch as C, or C♭, which is the same pitch as a B. C♭ can be found in the G♭ scale above.

THE CAPO
(For Guitar Players Only)

Guitar players often use a capo, usually a rubber-covered metallic bar that is clamped on the guitar neck to raise the key of a song. In addition to making it easy to change keys, the capo can make familiar chords sound fresher by giving your guitar a punchier, higher-pitched sound. Sometimes you have to retune the guitar a little, and if you use one on high fret positions it can muffle the sound of the bass notes.

Whether or not you use a capo, it is useful to understand

how transposition works. This is especially true if you play with bassists or piano players who do not use capos. They want to know that the song is in the key of D, not that it's in the key of C with the capo at the second fret.

FOLK SONGS

Literally speaking, folk songs are defined as songs that are passed along from one generation to another without the use of written music. Traditionally they were found in families or among particular social groups or tribes. No one knows who actually wrote these folk songs, and in many cases they were changed so much from one generation to the next that they might well have been unrecognizable to the original author or authors. Often folk songs were written in A form, containing only verses. If a chorus was present, it was often more like a refrain, a simple line or two that repeated after the verse, rather than a full-blown separate musical part.

◆ THE MODES

Many folk songs utilize scales that relate back to the Greek modes. The C major scale, CDEFGABC, is known as the ionian mode. If you start and end on D, the mode is known as the Dorian mode. Below is a chart of the various modes.

C D E F G A B C	Ionian mode
D E F G A B C D	Dorian mode
E F G A B C D E	Phrygian mode
F G A B C D E F	Lydian mode
G A B C D E F G	Mixolydian mode
A B C D E F G A	Aeolian mode
B C D E F G A B	Locrian mode

Notice that the half steps are marked in bold type. The half steps represent a distance of one fret on the guitar. If

we turn to the piano there are no black keys between the notes E and F and B and C.

Dorian Mode

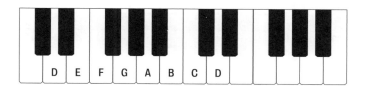

Phrygian Mode

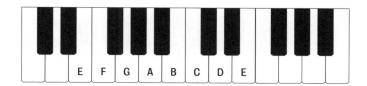

Lydian Mode

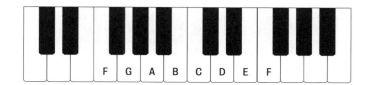

Mixolydian Mode

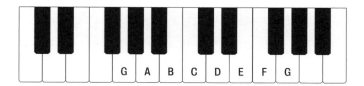

Aeolian Mode

Locrian Mode

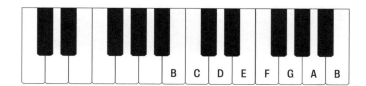

MODES

Dorian

Phrygian

Lydian

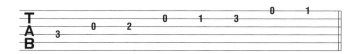

Mixolydian

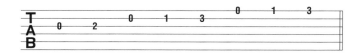

Aeolian

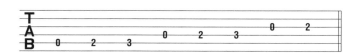

Locrian

⓭ "I Will Never See Her Again"

```
Am              G       Am
My love came to visit me on Monday.

G       Am
Tuesday, she was gone.

C       G       Am
I will never see her again, no.

C       G       Am
I will never see her again.
```

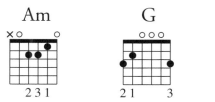 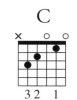

If you look at the melody, you will notice that there are only five notes used in this song. Five-note scales are called pentatonic scales, and are often utilized in teaching music to children on recorders or simple marimbas.

But what identifies this tune as a "folk song"? The simple, almost nostalgic nature of the melody is one factor. Another is the modal nature of the tune. There is a historical nature to songs written in folk song style that conjures up earlier, simpler times. Because we live in a complex and sophisticated world, there isn't really a way to write contemporary folk songs. It is possible, however, to write songs in a sort of parallel style that brings folk songs to mind.

Another aspect of folk songs is that they tend to be performed in a non-dramatic style, where the song tells the story. The performer is simply the vehicle for telling the story, rather than the focus of the audience's attention. In pop folk songs, some of the stylistic musical and lyrical elements are maintained, but because the focus *is* on the

◈ 13 "I Will Never See Her Again"

My love came to vis - it me on Mon - day.

Tues - day, she was gone. I will nev - er see her a -

gain, _____ no. I will nev - er see her a - gain.

"I Will Never See Her Again"

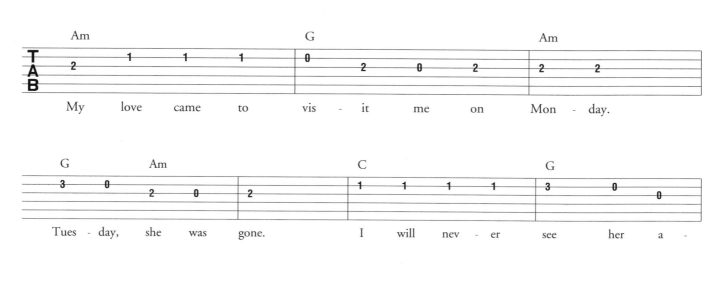

My love came to vis - it me on Mon - day.

Tues - day, she was gone. I will nev - er see her a -

gain, _____ no. I will nev - er see her a - gain.

singer, and the audience is a large one, the song is performed in much the manner that pop songs are. In other words, entertainment values become a primary focus of the performance.

WALTZ TIME (T)

Almost everything we have discussed thus far has been in $\frac{4}{4}$ time. In $\frac{4}{4}$ time the unit of time is the quarter note, and there are four beats for each bar of music. Although a tremendous amount of popular music is written in $\frac{4}{4}$ time, it is also possible to write in $\frac{3}{4}$, $\frac{5}{4}$, $\frac{6}{8}$, etc. To demonstrate $\frac{3}{4}$ time, let's try a song I wrote some years ago called "Take This Letter." There are two things that you should observe in this song. First of all, the song is in $\frac{3}{4}$, or waltz time. This means that there are three beats for each bar of music. The second thing I want to mention is that the chord progression goes I V IV, instead of the I IV V progression that is more common. This is called retrogression, or, in effect, moving backward. Here is the song:

◆⑭ "Take This Letter"

D / / / / / / /G / / Em / /
Take this letter across the sea.

A / / / / / / G / / D /
Send it where my love will be.

/ / / / / / / /G / Em /
I'll write to her, in a few short lines,

/ A / / / / /G / / D / /
To tell her of my lonesome times.

THE HIGH LONESOME SOUND

Another sort of country song, kind of halfway between mountain string band music and the modern bluegrass style, is the old folk song "Little Maggie." The "high lonesome sound" that is so much a part of bluegrass music comes from singing melodies in the high register, often

with tenor vocal parts that are pitched even higher than the lead singer's part. The song also uses the I bVII chord progression that is common in bluegrass and folk music. In the key of C this progression is C B♭ C; in the key of G it is G F G.

◆⑮ "Little Maggie"

D   C
Yonder stands little Maggie,

          D   C   D
With a dram glass in her hand.

                              C
She is drinking away her troubles,

          D   A   D
Over courting some other man.

Notice the high harmony vocal on the CD. Some people refer to country music and bluegrass as "white man's blues." This is intended to indicate that this music can also be soulful and expressive.

FOLK ROCK

Folk rock is music that has a rock beat but, whether because of the lyric content, the style of singing or the chord progressions, has a folk element as well. It isn't really the melody that defines the style. It is possible to take a folk song in $\frac{4}{4}$ time and add drums and heavy electric bass to transform a traditional song into a rock song. It is more common to utilize songs that are related to folk music (because they have a social message or because the vocal style of the artist sounds more like folk music than rock or pop) and add the rock beat to make the songs danceable, or close enough to allow for airplay. On the accompanying CD we will demonstrate how this is done. Dylan's relatively early recordings are classic folk rock recordings, as were the recordings of Dylan's songs by the Byrds.

ROCK 'N' ROLL

There are a tremendous number of rock musical subgenres. It would be impossible to cover them all in a single book lest the book become the size of a dictionary. But rock certainly includes the following sub-styles:

- Soft rock
- Hard rock
- '50s rock
- Heavy metal
- Punk
- New Wave
- Grunge
- Middle-of-the-road pop-rock
- Country rock
- Folk rock
- Jazz-rock, sometimes called fusion
- Industrial or techno rock
- Worldbeat-inflected rock

There are also rock-related styles that involve rhythm as a major part of the sound, like soul music, blues or hip-hop. One could say that these styles have some interchange with rock music, but aren't, strictly speaking, rock styles.

We can make a few generalizations about rock. Some of the categories above, for example, are self-defining. Country rock contains rock rhythms but country vocal inflections, and utilizes such "country" instruments as fiddle, pedal steel guitar and banjo. Folk rock is "folk" in the sense that the subjects of the songs are folk-oriented. Folk rock songs may be about political events, like Stephen Stills's "For What It's Worth," and some of the instruments usually identified with folk music, like acoustic guitars or twelve-string guitars, are often part of the sound. Punk rock typically has an angry tinge and uses a limited number of chords. The objective is to get across a certain

rawness of musical style and to vent anger at the prevailing social system.

Whether rock is of the hard or soft variety is generally dictated by the singer's vocal emphasis, together with the intensity, or lack of it, of the bass and drums.

GOSPEL AND CONTEMPORARY CHRISTIAN MUSIC

Traditional gospel music is strictly devotional. If contemporary or popular subjects enter into the lyrics, they are generally discussed in terms of God's love. In the case of black gospel music there have been occasional forays into contemporary politics, usually in the form of descriptions of racial injustice or inequality. These subjects are also broached in terms of Christian morality. Black gospel music almost invariably has a particular piano groove that immediately identifies the style of the song as a gospel song. Although there are black gospel groups that utilize the guitar for accompaniment, notably the Dixie Hummingbirds, typically the piano is where the gospel groove originates, with the organ running a close second. The vocal range of many black gospel singers is spectacular, so you can throw out the rules about songs having a limited vocal range. Low bass singers are a feature of gospel quartets, and the use of high falsetto parts is also quite common.

White gospel music has less of a rhythmic groove, although more modern versions of the idiom tend to show African-American influences. The feature of traditional "camp meeting" gospel music that is most obvious is four-part vocal harmony. Pop-country groups like the Statler Brothers or the Oak Ridge Boys show these influences.

Contemporary Christian music adopts a soft rock approach to the music. Acoustic guitar is often the featured instrument, and the rhythm sections tend to be somewhat restrained in intensity. Some of the artists in this idiom, like Amy Grant or Michael W. Smith, have crossed over into mainstream pop music. The lyrics of their songs tend to be less directly religious, but to those who are familiar with the music the notion of love is usually taken to mean God's love, rather than the sort of sexual intimacy favored by rock writers. The subjects of these songs tend to be home life, family, personal growth and revelations brought about through prayer.

SOUL MUSIC

Soul music is a kind of fusion between the musical elements of gospel and blues. The singers tend to perform in a very emotional style that utilizes their high registers. Screams, howls and moans are characteristic of the style. As with gospel music, you can anticipate that the artist will have a fairly spectacular vocal range, especially at the high end.

The subject most commonly dealt with in soul is romance. Failed love, yearnings for love and both successful and unsuccessful relationships are all grist for the soul music mill. There is usually a strong emphasis on the rhythm section, especially the bass and drums. Occasionally the songs spill over into such issues as life in the ghetto, war or other topics as seen through the prism of the black experience.

RAP

Rap is an extremely influential contemporary music style. It was born in the late 1970s in The Bronx, New York. The original impetus for rap was the work of some pioneering disc jockeys such as Cool Herc. These DJs used turntables as musical instruments, manipulating them to make the stylus go backward and forward on the surface of the record to repeat sounds or phrases rhythmically; this style was called "scratching." The sound created by such use of the turntables became part of the rhythmic foundation of the songs.

Originally rap was part of the hip-hop culture that included such things as break dancing and graffiti tagging. Partly because of the attempt to censor lyrics that more conservative elements felt were immoral or advocated the use of drugs or violence, gangsta rap has risen to the fore as an important and successful pop music style.

Rap uses extensive sampling, in which parts of songs from existing recordings are integrated electronically into new songs. These samples are sometimes undisguised, such as James Brown's scream. Other ways of using samples are to reprocess them so that they are difficult to recognize. In the section of the book called "The Money" we will discuss the economics of sampling.

Some rap artists talk right on the beat, but the more creative ones play with the rhythm, moving ahead of or behind the beat in much the same way that jazz musicians perform.

POP MUSIC

Pop music without some reference to rock scarcely exists today, but there are still a few singers, like Tony Bennett or a number of cabaret artists such as Maureen McGovern or Amanda McBroom, whose songs hark back to an earlier era of music, and yet retain enough aspects of current musical style not to seem dated.

The difference between rock and pop music is largely a difference in the approaches to rhythm and harmony. Rhythm is de-emphasized in pop music, and harmony, on the other hand, tends to be lush and thick. Pop songs utilize many more chords, as well as more elaborate extensions of these chords. For example, instead of a C chord you might find a C9 chord. Below is a chart of various chord extensions. I have given each chord as a variation of a C chord. Remember that when you transpose a song from one key to another all of the notes indicated in the chord name, such as C minor7♭5, will be the same in the new key. In other words if we are in the key of C and the chord indicated is a C minor7♭5 chord, the chord in the key of G will be a G minor7♭5.

CHORD	OTHER SYMBOLS FOR THE SAME CHORD	NOTES
C suspended 4	Csus4	CFG
C sixth	C6	CEGA
C minor 6	Cm6	CE♭GA
C diminished 7th	C dim., C°7	CE♭G♭A
C augmented 7th	C+7, Caug.7	CEG♯B♭
C major7flat5	CM7b5, CM7+	CEG♭B
C major7	Cmaj7, CΔ, CM7	CEGB
C7	Cdominant 7	CEGB♭
C minor7	Cm7, C-7	CE♭GB♭
C7flat5	C7♭5	CEG♭B♭
C minor7flat5	Cm7♭5, C°7	CE♭G♭B♭
C ninth	C9	CEGB♭D
C minor9	Cm9	CE♭GB♭D
C eleventh	C11	CEGB♭DF
C thirteenth	C13	CEGB♭DFA
C minor thirteenth	Cmi13	CE♭GB♭DFA

STANDARDS

Broadway show tunes and pop songs of the 1930s and '40s tended to use lush chord harmonies and rather complex melodies. Many of these tunes move from one key to another in different parts of the song, and many of the chords used in these styles of music have relatively few three-note chords. Many of the chords in the chart above are commonly used in these sorts of songs.

CHILDREN'S SONGS

There are several different genres of children's music. The type of songs that will be appropriate for these genres varies according to the musical styles involved, and the specific audience that the song is directed toward.

The first question to answer is, for what age group is the song intended? Songs for very young children must have a limited vocal range, and must be simple and catchy. These songs are often written in the A form, that is, with a single melody repeated throughout. Children under the ages of about ten or twelve are typically a non-rock audience, so the songs that are appropriate are often simplified versions of folk songs.

Children who are a bit older, say eleven to fourteen years old, are generally already fans of rock music, so writing songs for that age group more of a simplified or condensed version of rock songs.

Another aspect of this genre is that many of the songs intended for young children also need to appeal to adults. Usually it is the parents (often pressured by their children) who are the actual purchasers of the music. Parents often are extremely concerned that songs carry a positive message for their kids. This means that the songs might stress things from a more benevolent point of view. I remember a song that I once heard called "I'm Not Small." The message of this song is that it is ok for a child not to be the size of an adult. Other such songs might refer to tasks that a child is unable to do, or to making friends with kids who are different than you are (by gender, color or general inclinations). Another example of this sort of song is the song "Don't Laugh At Me," by Steve Seskin and Allen Shamblin.

Recently, children's songs have even leaned toward social activism—not wasting things, protecting the environment, and in general helping to create a better world for everyone. More traditional folk songs often involve games or dances. It is quite common for kids' songs to be written in a sing-along format, in such a way that a whole class or roomful of kids can sing the songs together.

Another style of children's songs is the production-number song, usually found in the musical score of Disney or Disney-like films. Many of these songs are like simplified Broadway songs, with clever lyrics and catchy melodies. More than any other kind of kids' songs, the Disney formula is especially designed to appeal to the parents of middle-class kids.

In Canada there are a number of television shows that feature performers who sing, like Fred Penner. Some of these songs are syndicated on cable television in the United States as well. *Sesame Street* and its various offshoots and imitators also feature quite a bit of music. Raffi is another Canadian performer who has built a very successful performing and recording career in children's music.

Recently some older rockers have begun recording songs for young people; if you want to go back to the source, '50s rock is easy to sing, and danceable. As such it can be very appealing to young children.

Following is "Don't Whine," a song written by Dave and Helene Van Manen. The Van Manens write and perform many songs designed to help children develop a positive self-image. The lyric is designed to appeal to parents as well as kids. The person singing the song recalls how he too irritated his parents at times. This information is

presented in a light and humorous way, so that children won't be annoyed by the lyric. Adults, of course, will love it.

The music printed is a sketch used on the recording date, without lyrics.

16 "D o n ' t   W h i n e"
Words and music by Dave Van Manen

Once when I was eight or maybe nine
I saw this baseball glove and I wanted it to be mine
So I asked my Mom to buy it
I said Mom, it's really cool.
You see. It's signed by Mickey Mantle
And it's 100% rawhide leather
And it's endorsed by the New York Yankees
And I really want it, Mom
Please Mom, can I get it,
Come on, Mom, PLEASE
(She said)

CHORUS
Don't whine, don't whine
If I've told you once, I've told you a hundred times
Don't whine, don't whine
Just talk to me, but please don't whine!
I remember once, my Mom said, take a bath
It's been over a week since you had your last
But taking a bath didn't fit my evening plans
So I said, Mom, I don't want to take a bath
I have plans. Billie is coming over and we were gonna
Play in my room. Then we're gonna go to his house.
Mom, I don't want to take a bath
Come on, Mom, PLEASE
(She said)

"Don't Whine"

CHORUS

Now I'm all grown up with kids of my own
Just the other day they said, Dad, we don't wanna go
   home.
We want to go to a movie,
And then we want to get something to eat
Oh, come on, Dad
You told us last week you'd take us to see
   a movie
And it's boring at home
Yeah, we're at home like all the time
Dad, please, come on Dad PLEASE
   (I said)

CHORUS

JAZZ

There are numerous kinds of jazz, and they are quite different from one another. The differences are mostly in rhythm and harmony, although even the way melodies are addressed varies in different genres of jazz.

The earliest jazz styles developed alongside ragtime and blues. We usually use the name Dixieland or New Orleans jazz to indicate these styles. Jazz is more of an instrumental style than a vocal one, but there have always been numerous excellent jazz singers. Consequently, composers like Duke Ellington worked with lyricists to broaden the appeal of their compositions.

Since jazz is a rather complex form, and there are books larger than this one that specifically deal with musical and artistic aspects of jazz. I will only offer a few brief ideas about jazz in this section.

17 DIXIELAND CHORD PROGRESSION

One of the most popular chord progressions in Dixieland jazz and in ragtime is I, VI7, II7, V7, I. In the key of C these chords are C, A7, D7, G7 C. If you look up the key identification chart on page 47, you will see that in the key of G these chords will be G, E7, A7, D7 and G. Some well-known songs that use this chord progression include "Ja-da," "Charleston" and the country-bluegrass standard "Salty Dog."

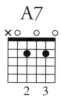

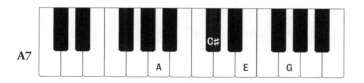

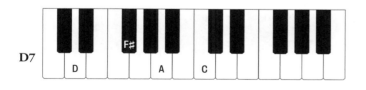

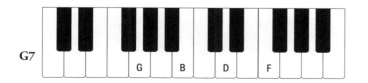

SWING

Swing bands are much larger ensembles than are found in Dixieland. Much of Dixieland is "ear" music, meaning that it is possible to improvise the parts without a great deal of technical musical training. Since swing uses groups of horns playing together, it is pretty much necessary to be able to read music to play in swing band. Rhythmically, swing has much more of a walking bass, four chords to the bar in $\frac{4}{4}$ time type of feel than Dixieland, which is sometimes called "two beat." On the CD you will find some brief examples of these musical styles.

BEBOP AND BEYOND

In the 1940s a group of mostly young African-American musicians started experimenting with much more complex harmony parts. They took jazz tunes and pop standards and substituted complex chords, such as minor seventh chords with a flatted fifth, for the original chords of tunes.

Singers developed complex musical vocal styles such as scat singing to go with the innovations of bebop. Many of these songs used syllables instead of lyrics, so they do not really fit into the context of a book about songwriting as such.

Later jazz developments include jazz-rock, fusion, chamber jazz and jazz-funk music patterns. These are mostly not vocal styles.

POP-JAZZ

Contemporary jazz singers (and players) like John Pizzarelli, Norah Jones and Diana Krall bridge the gap between contemporary jazz and pop music. They utilize jazz harmonies and phrasing, but integrate these styles into a pop music format that is more listenable to the average person than more traditional jazz singing and playing.

CHORD USE

The more you get to know about harmony, the more you realize that there are virtually an infinite number of chord choices that can be used in a particular song. In addition to all of the extended chords described above, it is possible to use chords as substitutes for other chords to create even richer harmonic patterns. For exa mple, let's take a standard sort of blues in the key of D. The chords will be D, D7, G, G7 and A7.

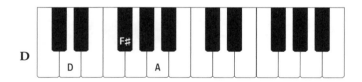

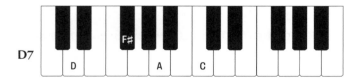

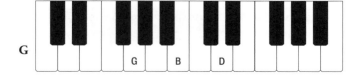

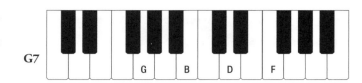

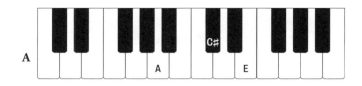

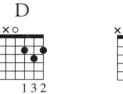 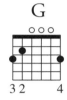

  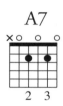

18 "Goin' Up the Country"

D   D7 G G7   D D7
Goin' up the country, singin' nothin' but you.
    G   G7   D
Yes, I'm goin' up the country, singin' nothin' but you.
   A
If you don't hear me callin',

G   D G D A7
I don't know what I'm goin' to do.

Try the following chords instead:

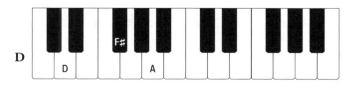

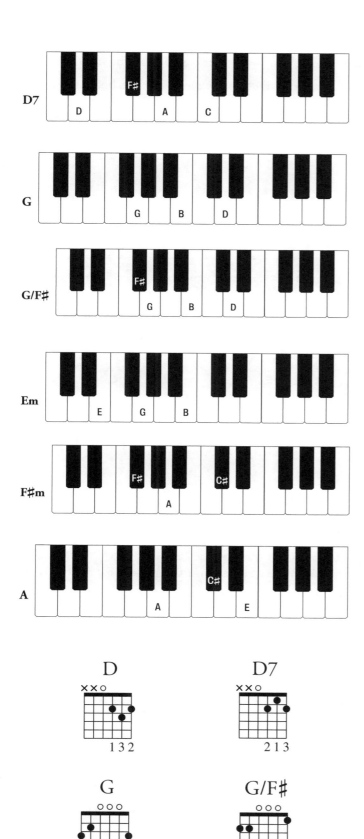

Em   F#m   A

D   D7   G   G/F# Em   D   D7
Goin' up the country, singin'   nothin' but you.

      G   F#m   Em   G   F#m   Em D   D7
Yes, I'm goin' up the country, singin' nothin' but you.

      A   G   F#m
If you don't hear me callin',

G   F#m   D Em F#m   G
I don't know what I'm goin' to do.

Modifying one set of chords by using others is called chord substitution. The final arbiter of whether a chord can be substituted for another chord is your own ear. You can also go back and look at the chart of scales. The D scale contains the notes D E F# G A B C# D. The G chord has the notes G, B and D. The E minor chord contains the notes E, G and B. Chords that contain many of the same common tunes can often be substituted for one another.

When you use chord substitutions, the melody usually remains similar to the melody used with the original chord. You haven't changed the melody; what you have changed is the harmonic structure of the song. However, these changes will make the melody appear to change, especially if the chord substitutions contain more lush harmonies, such as major chords.

Chord substitutions can be very effective in songs that are lengthy, because the appearance of having the melody change can provide a welcome relief to the listener, who otherwise might become bored with the song.

WRITING FROM BASS LINES

Just as a chord progression, for better or worse, can result in leading a writer into a melody, a bass line can provide the same result. Below is a bass line in the key of C, diagrammed for guitar and piano. Close the book and try to visualize a melody derived from this bass line, and you will see one possibility.

Bass Line

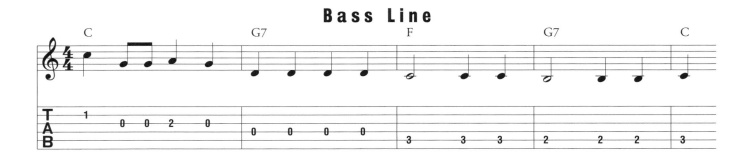

This melody can also be found on the CD that comes with the book.

    C   G
I—— want to see you soon, soon as soon can be

This is how the first part of the melody could sound. We can then proceed with the melody without any concentration on the bass line. One result might be:

C   G
I—— want to see you soon, soon as soon can
F   G   C
Be. What I wanted to be, is to be with you soon.

A more sophisticated way of writing from bass lines involves using descending bass lines. For example play a G chord with a G as the bass note, followed by a D major chord with an F# in the bass, and an Em with an E in the bass.

🔷19 "I Want to See You Soon"

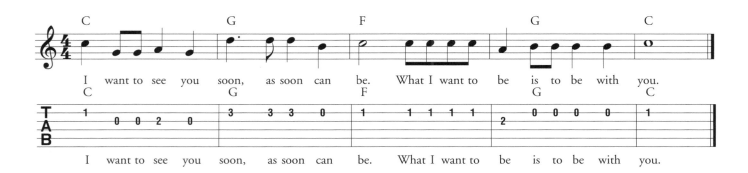

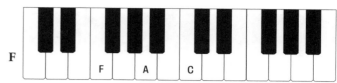

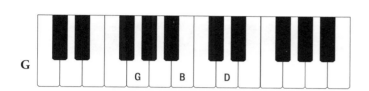

 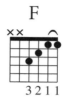

POWER CHORDS AND PARTIAL CHORDS

In heavy metal music it is quite common to play two-note "chords" that are sometimes called power chords. These stark sounds are very exciting, and they sound ominous and dramatic.

The opening line of a power chord-driven song might be:

Goin' down so slow, want you to know, it's over now.

From this beginning line the song could open up into more conventional chord patterns, or you can continue to explore the use of these intervals instead.

We've now explored a variety of musical styles and ways of beginning to write songs. In the next chapter we'll look at the use of rhythms, especially the notion of writing aided by such technological advances as sequencers, drum machines or MIDI.

◆20 Power Chords

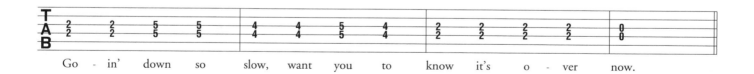

Go - in' down so slow, want you to know it's o - ver now.

CHAPTER 7 RESOURCES

Jimmy Webb's *Tunesmith* and Stephen Citron's *Songwriting: A Complete Guide to the Craft* are good references for tips on writing melodies. Both of the Rooksby books mentioned in the previous chapter apply to this chapter as well.

You've Got Rhythm

In many ways rhythm is the foundation of virtually all American popular music. Rhythm also provides the ultimate glue that makes popular music so appealing. In hip-hop music it is not just the foundation, but really half of the house where the music lives.

Many popular musicians have extraordinary rhythmic abilities, even thought it is more of a natural than a studied thing. Let's start off by introducing a few basic concepts about rhythm.

Music is written in some sort of time signature. There are two numbers at the left-hand side of the musical staff. If these numbers are $\frac{4}{4}$, it means that the basic unit of time is a quarter note (indicated by the bottom 4), and that there are four of these notes in each bar of music (indicated by the top 4). Therefore $\frac{3}{4}$ time means that there are three beats in each bar of music, and each of those is a quarter note in duration; $\frac{7}{8}$ time means that there are seven eighth notes in a single bar of music.

ACCENTS

The musical beats can be accented in various ways. For example, in $\frac{4}{4}$ time, it is possible to accent the first and third beats of the measure, or the second and fourth beats. Most blues songs have the accent on the second and fourth beats; many folk songs or older country song contain accents on the first and third beats of the measure. It is also possible to have music that doesn't contain strong accents. If you watch popular musicians playing music, they often tap their feet on the second and fourth beats of the bar. There are also musicians who seem to keep all four beats of the bar. At a fast tempo this is not a good idea, because it will mostly make your feet tired rather than help you to keep time.

In $\frac{3}{4}$ time it is customary to tap only on the first beat of each measure, such as 1 2 3 , 1 2 3. etc.

CUT TIME

Sometimes music is written in $\frac{4}{4}$ time, but it is meant to be played quite fast. This is indicated by the symbol ₵ with a line drawn through it. This stands for "cut time," or "common time." Be sure to tap cut time with two beats, not four, or your foot may literally be about ready to fall off by the time the tune is finished.

RHYTHMIC SUBTLETY

It is common for musicians to exaggerate rhythms and rhythmic accents. This can become quite tiresome to the listener. It is rarely necessary to maintain a frantic rhythmic figure in an entire song, although there may be specific songs where this technique does work. It is appealing to save that impetus, for example, for the choruses of the song.

The worst scenario of all is to do song after song with no break for the listener from insistent rhythmic patterns. If the music is used in a musical environment when people are dancing to every song, you may want to throw this piece of advice out the window. However, what works in a live music situation may not be equally effective on a recorded piece of music.

To develop a sharper rhythmic sense, try singing songs on the beat, in front of the beat or behind the beat. When you feel comfortable doing this, you will find that your writing will start to become less rhythmically predictable. Start out with something really simple, like the opening phrase of "Three Blind Mice." The rhythms are indicated by the slash (/) over each word.

◆ 21 "Three Blind Mice"

/   /   /   / /   /   / /
Three blind mice, three blind mice
/   /   / / /   /   /
See how they run, see how they run

Now take the same lyric, but change the way that you sing the melody, singing the notes behind the beat, following the slashes.

/   /   / / /   /   / /
Three blind mice, three blind mice

/   /   / / /   /   / /
See how they run, see how they run

Now try the same phrase, singing before the beat:

/   /   / / /   /   /   /
Three blind mice, three blind mice
/   /   / / / /   / /
See how they run, see how they run

Another rhythmic exercise that is fun is to take a song that is written in a particular meter, say $\frac{4}{4}$, and change it to another meter, such as $\frac{3}{4}$. Below is the music for the old chestnut "Go Tell Aunt Rhody." It is written in $\frac{4}{4}$ time. Try it in $\frac{3}{4}$ time:

◆ 22 "Go Tell Aunt Rhody"

/// / /   /   / / / / / / / / / / /   / / / / / /
Go tell Aunt Rhody, Go tell Aunt Rhody,
/// / / /   / / / / / /   / / /   / / / /   // HOLD
Go tell Aunt Rhody, the old grey goose is dead.

Try it on your own. If you're having trouble, turn to the CD and listen to the song in $\frac{3}{4}$ time.

It is also possible to change songs to other meters, such as $\frac{6}{8}$, $\frac{5}{4}$, etc. Some songs are so indelibly tied to a specific rhythm that they will never sound even remotely correct to you in a different rhythmic scheme. I think you will be surprised how many songs *can* survive this sort of treatment.

DRUMMERS AND BASS PLAYERS

Drummers and bass players play a key role in virtually every area of popular music. Sometimes a songwriter will bring a song into a rehearsal and it simply doesn't gel with the rhythm section. There are a number of possible reasons for this happening. Here are a few possibilities:

1) There are so many words in the song that it is impossible for the rhythm section to find a groove without interfering with the lyric.

2) The bass player seems to feel that he or she is the lead guitarist. Rather than supporting what the drummer is doing, some bassists insist on playing endless solos. This leaves the drummer alone in the role of timekeeping, with possible assistance from the rhythm guitarist.

3) The drummer and bass player play with a different time feel. Some players tend to play right in front of the beat, others lay back just behind it. If both of these viewpoints is present in your rhythm section, the songs will never find a good groove. Most listeners aren't aware of such subtleties, but they might find your band hard to dance to, or even to listen to.

If you are playing in a band, be sure that the bass player and drummer lock in together. This will be most obvious in the relationship between the bass drum and the bass.

ACCENTS

In a $\frac{4}{4}$ bar of music, it is possible to place the accent on the first and third beats of a bar, or on the second and fourth beats. Music that has been influenced by soul music or blues is generally accented on the second and fourth beats. Some older folk songs and country songs have more of an accent on the first and third beats, or they may have relatively little rhythmic accents at all. "Go Tell Aunt Rhody" in its original form in $\frac{4}{4}$ time is a song that really hasn't got much of a rhythmic accent, except possibly a slight emphasis on the first beat of each measure.

Examine the melodies you have written. If you find that you always place your accents in the same way, it is a good idea to deliberately attempt to write something that uses different accent patterns. If you are unsure how to do this, try to write in a specific style, such as a blues, where it is obvious that the accent will be in a particular place (in this case on the second and fourth beats of the bar.)

Writing in different rhythmic patterns may open your eyes to styles of music that have previously been a mystery to you.

RELATING RHYTHMS TO LYRICS

There is more than one way to deal with rhythms in relation to lyrics. The most obvious thing is to follow the thrust of the lyric in the rhythm. In other words, if you are telling a touching love story, it is generally inappropriate to use really choppy or aggressive rhythms. On the other hand, if you are writing a rap about a drive-by shooting, then you are probably going to stick with a hard and insistent rhythm pattern.

It is also possible to have the rhythm work in opposition to the lyric content of a song. Your love song might actually have a funky and insistent drum part. Part of what you need to consider is the question of who is performing the song. I can imagine a singer like Madonna doing exactly what we have just described—fitting a very insistent rhythm to a rather tender story line.

The key to these decisions is to try to be objective. Listen to your song on tape. It shouldn't appear ridiculous, nor should it be so obvious that the listener knows right away what will be in store.

RELATING RHYTHMS AND MELODIES

It is possible for rhythm to relate to melodies in the same

way. That is, they can follow the pattern of the melody: a gentle melody with a gentle rhythm, or an emotional melody with a harder, more insistent rhythm.

Remember that you have three ingredients of the song itself: the words, the melody and the rhythm. They need to fit together; if not, you need to change whatever elements seem to be sticking out and making the song unconvincing.

23 SYNCOPATION

Syncopation occurs when the accents are placed on the off beats of a song rather than played directly on the beat. In my experience, many musicians have more trouble reading rhythms than they do notes. If you have played an instrument for a while, chances are that you will pretty well know where the notes are on your instrument. When you see rhythms that seem strange to you (at least on paper), you are left without any feeling of security about executing them. Knowing where the notes are does not help you to understand the rhythms.

Let's take a jazz waltz pattern. Waltzes are in $\frac{3}{4}$ time, and usually the beats are very even as 1 2 3. Each note or chord will come right on the beat.

In a jazz waltz the notes will come on the first beat of the bar, on the and, or after the second beat, and on the third beat.

If the beats are / / / , the notes will come as shown below with the syllable Da. Da——da da. The notes here are dotted quarter note, eighth note and quarter note. The same figure could be written as a quarter note tied

to an eighth note, followed by an eighth note and then a quarter note.

Similar approaches can be taken to playing rhythms on the piano and guitar, instead of playing all the chords evenly as quarter notes or eighth notes.

Syncopation is a very exciting addition to your arsenal of rhythmic figures. Be careful not to overuse it. When syncopations are used over and over again they create a sort of jerky or jumpy feeling to the rhythm, which can become irritating. After a while the listener may lose contact with where the one of each bar is.

WORLD MUSIC

More and more musicians are listening to music from all over the world. Even the most cursory attempts at listening to world music will reveal what appear to be "odd" rhythms. These are rhythms that are found in different parts of the world that are not part of American popular music. Such rhythms as $\frac{7}{8}$ and $\frac{5}{4}$ time are common in Greek music. "Odd" rhythms are also common to the music of Africa, the Arab world and India. The chapter on instrumental music will discuss some of these styles.

CHAPTER 8 RESOURCES

If you are interested in experimenting with different rhythms, check out music folios in the drum and percussion sections of your local music store.

Many computer owners are using the program called Garage Band, which enables the songwriter to utilize a rhythm section to play along with her original tunes. With this program the songwriter can also create rhythm loops, which provide a rhythm section for the writer.

Mark Phillips has written a book to aid in rhythmic sight-reading called *Understanding Rhythm.*

Another, much more advanced book is Peter Hampton Phillips's *The Rhythm Book.*

The Music Minus One play-along records and similar projects available from Jamey Aebersold will also help you to understand rhythms.

See the appendix for the addresses for these resources.

Putting the Words and the Music Together, and the Art of Collaboration

It is very difficult to explain exactly how words and music go together, but it is fairly simple to listen to a song and understand that this process has magically occurred. Certain aspects of combining the two elements are relatively obvious. Below are a few guidelines:

1) Is the lyric easy to sing, or do the words and the melody seem to bump against one another?

2) Are the styles compatible? You wouldn't expect to hear a Latin rhythm set to a country song. Unless there is some intelligent reason for this to happen, you should avoid doing it. An intelligent reason might be that the song is, let's say, about a country singer stranded in Bolivia, or that the song is set on the Texas-Mexico border, as the country standard "El Paso" is.

3) Do the words and music work together, or is one getting in the way of the other? If the melody is complex and requires a huge vocal range, it may interfere with the delivery of the lyric. If the lyric uses a lot of consonants and the sheer sound of these words is unpleasant, it may be difficult to tailor a melody that works.

4) Is there a sense that one person could have written the song, even though it may have been written by two or even three writers working together? The words and the music should feel as though they were crafted together, even though in many cases they weren't.

STRATEGIES FOR REVISION

It is important that a writer retain some level of objectivity about his or her own work. Assuming that the same writer did both the words and the music, are you really satisfied with both? Most writers are stronger at either the words or the music. If you know from the very beginning that you are better at writing one or the other, you should be aware that you are going to have to do more revisions on the weaker part of your craft. In my own case I find it much easier to craft melodies than lyrics. I am perfectly capable of writing reasonably good lyrics, but I always know that it is going to take me far longer to come up with them than with melodies.

In many instances you may be able to discard a song, yet retain some portions of the melody or lyrics to use in another song. Often it takes some time after you have actually completed the work before you can reach that sort of decision. Another possibility is to use a collaborator to write whichever part of the song you feel is the weakest.

COLLABORATION

In traditional pop music, lyricists and composers were two separate groups of people. George Gershwin didn't write lyrics, and his brother Ira didn't write music. The same held true for many of the people who wrote Broadway shows. For every Irving Berlin or Cole Porter, who wrote both music and lyrics, there were several dozen Jerome Kerns, Carolyn Leighs, Harold Arlens, etc., who specialized in one or the other. There were a number of reasons for this. Broadway lyrics tend to be wordy and sophisticated, and it is not unusual for the writers to have to come up with virtually instant songs to throw into a show as it is going through its tryout phases in out-of-town venues. With two people working together, this process can be done in a quicker and more efficient way than if the same person is responsible for both aspects of the songs.

MODERN COLLABORATION

These days collaboration takes place for reasons other than expediency or strict specialization in lyrics or music. Some writers find it convenient and useful to bounce ideas off one another. Some writers are wonderful at coming up with concepts for songs, but don't do as well in the line-to-line drudgery of crafting verses. For some people, having another person around provides a form of discipline that ensures that they will work on the song rather than walk the dog, eat or answer the telephone.

Many of these contemporary collaborations cannot be conveniently split into the roles of one person doing the words and another the music. Both people might be sitting around a table playing guitars, or one might be playing guitar and the other one keyboards. Different people work in different ways. Sometimes a writer will come into a collaboration session with a specific idea, or even a song title. Other writers prefer to do it on the spot. One writer might set up a particular rhythm or melodic figure on the guitar or piano, while the other one throws out lyric lines.

No two people write the same way. Some people start with a concept and a hook, some write the chorus before writing the verse. Story songwriters may prefer to write with a sense of continuity, with a beginning, a middle and an ending, crafted consecutively.

TOGETHER OR SEPARATELY

Collaboration can be done with two or three people working in a room together, starting from scratch. Other collaborators may come in with a partially realized idea that they want help in refining or completing. Other writers don't actually work together on songs. One may give the other a complete lyric and ask them to then create an appropriate melody. A writer with melodic skills might come in with a completed melody on tape or in musical notation, and the other writer may then construct his lyric according to that melody.

This sort of collaboration can actually take place at a distance, with occasional e-mail or telephone conferences on whether each writer is happy with the direction of the song. It is important that collaboration proceed on a business-like basis, and that the parties have an agreement on who owns what rights.

THE BUSINESS OF COLLABORATION

It is important that you and your collaborator or collaborators have a business agreement that specifies who has the right to do what, and who owns the song that you will be writing. In most instances it is a good idea for collaborations to work on a 50-50 basis.

The core of such an agreement has to be good faith. In

other words, the partners should not nitpick each other. In one instance you may have written 60% of the words and 30% of the music. I am talking here about a long-term agreement, not about a single song collaboration. If circumstances create the need to collaborate on a particular song with someone whom you will probably not work with again, then you may want to parcel the song out according to the work done. This is particularly true when a writer has basically completed a song, but is stuck on a particular part, like the bridge. Under such circumstances a 2/3-1/3 split might make sense.

Similarly someone who threw in a melodic fragment or a small portion of the lyric might be entitled to, say, 20% of the song. It's really up to the writers and their sense of fairness.

An agreement between collaborators should also state what will happen if one party doesn't like what the other has done. This is fairly easy to do if one person is writing the words and the other the music, but it is much more complex if it isn't entirely clear as to who wrote what. Under the latter circumstances the easiest thing to do might be to abandon the song. Even this may lead to trouble, because of the possibility that the song may have one or two really good lines that one writer or the other wants to use in another song.

DEMOS

There will be a more comprehensive look at song demos later in the book, but co-writing provides some potentially useful options for making demos. Often one writer may be a good singer, another a good musician. By pooling these talents you can make a good demo of your song keep your costs down. These days it is possible that one writer has a home studio and good technical skills. This is another way of making better and cheaper song demos.

PRODUCERS AND ARTISTS AS COLLABORATORS

Some artists and producers like collaborating with other songwriters. This can be great for a writer, because clearly artists and producers have access to making records. Garth Brooks, for example, has collaborated with a number of writers.

The key question in this situation is whether the artist or producer is contributing an equal share to the collaboration. If he isn't, the writer may feel that he is not being treated fairly. More cynical writers may feel that that is the price they must pay to get their songs recorded. It is entirely up to you, but you should be aware of what the situation is.

BAND COLLABORATIONS

Many bands become quite confused about the nature of collaborations. Bass lines or drum figures are part of a musical arrangement, not the composition of a melody or the authoring of lyrics. If your bass player and drummer feel they helped "write" the song, the best thing to tell them is that they will share in the money from the band's gigs, and in the artist royalties from the recordings. Songwriting is not a matter of coming up with bass and drum parts or lead guitar lines. Those elements constitute the gravy for the song; the melody and lyrics are the meat and potatoes.

If the band is really a co-op group, with individuals who feel a great deal of loyalty to one another, then the logical solution is for the group to share in the publishing rights of the song. This is possible only if you haven't already signed a contract giving these rights up. We'll have more to say about such matters in later chapters.

MATTERS OF PERSONAL STYLE

If you expect to work on your collaborations in a face-to-face situation, there are some interpersonal aspects of working together that you need to consider. Here are a few:

1) Do you have a place where you are both comfortable working?

2) Is there some equality in the collaborative process? If one person has written forty-three hit songs and the other has never had a song recorded, the imbalance in the relationship may get on both people's nerves sooner or later. However, it is not unusual for older, skilled writers to develop a sort of mentoring relationship with younger songwriters. The younger writer may have more familiarity with younger people's musical tastes, and may have a higher energy level than a somewhat jaded veteran. This sort of collaboration can be mutually beneficial. Each person brings different skills to the party, and different contacts as well.

3) Are you both comfortable working at particular times of day? Some people really like working in the morning; some seem to function creatively only late at night; and some seem entirely indifferent to this question.

4) Do your personalities mesh? Some people are annoyingly positive or negative; some people are nags. Some people are incurably analytical, and others are great at doing the work but can't talk about it.

5) Do you have mutual musical and aesthetic interests? Some writers are primarily concerned with money, while others are more interested in writing songs that they personally like. Some people love specific musical styles and hate others. Can you work happily together?

REAL-LIFE COLLABORATIONS

There are two collaborations on the DVD that accompanies this book. The first is a three-way collaboration that includes Michael Kearsey, a versatile bass and guitar player; Halie Loren, a talented singer-songwriter from Eugene, Oregon; and me. Halie came in with most of her song finished but she felt that we needed to add a bridge to the song. As you can see from the chart, the song is in the key of G, and I immediately heard the bridge as moving to Em. This is what Halie brought in:

To reach out and touch
Like an enchanted child, I never had a chance

B SECTION
So sweet on the tongue
But now it's done
The aftertaste leaves something to be desired

CHORUS
Bitter fruit,
Bitter fruit.
Such a bitter fruit by design
A bitter fruit, and now it's mine.

VERSE
Everyone deserves it
And everyone can earn it
Or so the modern prophets lead us to believe
But the moment that you get it
There's a good chance you'll regret it
In that part of you that's longing to be free

B SECTION
Once that it's yours
You hunger for more
Until the dream is eating you up inside

CHORUS

(Here is the bridge we came up with, during the video shoot.)

BRIDGE

Sometimes the things we see
Aren't always what they seem
Sometimes the life that you desire
Should stay a dream
Because illusions never change
If you want them to remain
Without the changes that imperfect life will bring

CHORUS

Bitter fruit,
Bitter fruit
Such a bitter fruit by design
A bitter fruit. And now it's mine.

(TAG)

A bitter fruit most every time.

During the video we came up with the idea of not resolving the final chord, but going to the four chord (C) to create a feeling of uncertainty. Halie notes that she would like to change the word 'desire' in the bridge, to something else.

Notice how the feel is created by piano playing the lead, supported by guitar and electric bass. Some polishing is going to be necessary to complete the song, but it certainly represents a good start. Because Halie came in with 2/3 of the song complete, we probably got closer to a finished song in this collaboration, as you will soon see, than in the other tune.

The second tune on the video is a two-way collaboration I did with Michael Kearsey. Although we've done some playing together, we had never attempted to write a song

before. We went into the collaboration with a concept I had developed, which was to write a song that revolved around a list of clichés in current use. My idea was to make fun of these phrases. Here is the list that Michael and I came up with:

Awesome
Back in the day
Been there, done that
Branding
Building a buzz
Count on it
Dude!
Easy come, easy go
Go girl
Going green
Good point
Good to go
Got it
Have a nice day
I hear you
I know what you're saying
It's all good
It's a no-brainer
It's not rocket science
Keep it real
Monetize it
Put your hands together
Take it to the bank
Tell me something I don't know
That's a given
The best defense is a good offense
There you go again
Too much on my plate
Whatever
Whatever works
Who cares?
Win-win
Yawn
Yes we can (what?)

Michael felt that the direction we should go was to contrast these clichés with an older, calmer way of life. Here is what we came up with:

VERSE

Back in the day there was time to talk,
People used to say what was on their mind
Talk about books, talk about life
Remember Cousin Al and his beautiful wife.
But life goes on, you know what I mean?
Twitter, Facebook, digital scenes,
You can text your friends
Do they know what you say?
'Cause there's more to your life
Than a simple cliché.

CHORUS

Tell me something I don't know,
24/7, let it flow,
You got to build a buzz, you know what they say,
If it works for you, then have a nice day.

VERSE

Dad was a man who worried about taxes,
He worked a long week, long before faxes
Mom thought about people, and changing the world,
She worried and wondered since her days as a girl
And we text but don't talk,
We drive but don't walk
We still care as much
But we don't stay in touch
I hear children say
In a four-letter way
There's more to your life
Than a simple cliché.

You can read the music below or watch the DVD. This all evolved in an hour, and realistically if we wanted to do something with the song it would take some rewriting and probably some better coordination between the words and the music. Note that we haven't come up with a lyric hook to tie the song together. The phrase "a simple cliché" could work as a title, as might "have a nice day." Notice how different the feel is on this song, without the piano.

COLLABORATIONS ON THE INCLUDED DVD

"Bitter Fruit"

H. Loren, R. Weissman, M. Kearsey
©2010 Used by Permission

Note: It is difficult to explain how someone "hears" a bridge to a preexisting song. It is a combination of listening to the verse and chorus melody and trying to create a groove that is appropriate.

"A SIMPLE CLICHÉ"

WORDS AND MUSIC BY J. MICHAEL KEARSEY AND DICK WEISSMAN
©2010 USED BY PERMISSION

Note: In the third line of the verse, you can use either an Am chord or a C major 7th. You might want to transpose the song down from G to D or E if it is too high for your vocal.

CHAPTER 9 RESOURCES

Walter Carter wrote an entire book on the subject of collaboration. *The Songwriters Guide to Collaboration,* (Mix Books, 1997). It is my opinion that if you need to read an entire book on collaboration, then you may well be too distrustful of other people to be involved in a fruitful collaboration.

Keeping the Flame Alive

Everyone who writes songs—or for that matter, anyone who writes anything—has periods of fiery creativity where the computer (or the pencil) can't seem to write fast enough to follow his or her ideas. Unfortunately, the same thing holds true for periods of utter despair, when the writer can't seem to write anything that he or she likes, or can't even write anything at all.

It would be wonderful if there were a simple solution to this problem, some series of exercises, vacations, systems of meditation or prayer or anything else that could solve these problems. The truth is there isn't a specific solution for a loss of inspiration or energy. There are, however, things that you can do to create an environment that will enable you to write again.

DOING NOTHING

For many creative people the hardest thing to do is to do nothing. Take a few days off. Engage in some sort of activity that isn't normal for you. It might be hiking, gardening, mountain climbing, going to the beach, reading unrelated books, going to a concert by an artist who usually inspires you, or listening to different kinds of music. For some people, physical activity is something they don't normally do; others never allow themselves

time for mental activity that isn't directly related to song-writing. The most extreme form of "doing nothing" is to take a trip to a place that you have never been before. The phone won't ring, and you can just walk around and observe what people do. You might do what Tom T. Hall does and go to places like bars and coffeehouses and simply listen to the way people talk and what they have to say. It is best if you choose places that aren't your regular haunts.

MUSICAL CHANGES

If you play a musical instrument, try something that' new to you. I remember reading about a famous Nashville writer who was experiencing a serious dry spell. He told another writer about it, who taught him the G tuning for the guitar. Since this tuning involves retuning three strings, none of the normal chord formations apply. The writer had to simply experiment, following his ear and wherever his fingers would take him. He completed three songs almost immediately.

For guitar players, the G tuning, from lowest to highest string, is DGDGBD. Another interesting tuning, used for Celtic music but for other musical styles as well, is DADGAD. Tunings are just one way to scramble your writing deck. If you are a finger-style guitar player, try playing with a pick. You might even want to take some lessons from someone who is fluent in that style. If you are a pick-style player, try playing with your fingers. Another option is to study classical guitar, which is picked with the fingers, but in a very different way than fingerpicking country or folk-style guitar.

If you are a keyboard player, you can either learn a different style of playing or acquire a late-model electronic keyboard that has the capability of playing different sounds than those available on the one you currently own.

RETHINKING LYRICS

If you feel that your lyrics are in a rut you might try examining the subjects you usually write about. If you generally write romantic love songs, try to write something where the groove is the primary factor. If you write story songs, examine whether you are repeatedly telling the same story.

Many writers primarily write about themselves and their own experiences. Deliberately go outside your own experiences and friendship circles and write about something that has absolutely nothing to do with you. Don't prejudge what you are doing. Write songs about baseball, or politics or something based on a newspaper or magazine story. Try to put yourself into someone else's world.

COLLABORATORS AND RUTS

Just as you may become tired of your own work, it is possible to become too comfortable in a relationship with a particular collaborator. Some writers are too assertive, some too shy and reticent. Try to find someone who has an entirely different style than your usual collaborator or collaborators, and who has different work habits than the people you normally use. If you have always worked in

the morning, try working in the evening. If you've always worked at home, work in an office, or outdoors.

CAN YOU DO ANYTHING IF NOTHING WORKS?

Let's suppose you've tried quite a few of the methods suggested above and the results have been disastrous. You are now beginning to doubt whether you will ever write a song again. There are still some possibilities left for you.

One of the reasons many writers keep notebooks is so they can go to the notebook when inspiration seems to fail. Sometimes a writer finds a great idea for a new songburied in the remains of an unsuccessful song writtenweeks, months or even years earlier. Give up trying to write something new for a while, and become an editor rather than a writer.

Almost every songwriter has come up with good ideas, hooks, titles, choruses or verses that never found a home. See if it makes sense for you to weave different songs together, combining the best lines, melodies or choruses from your old songs to make new ones.

When writers are confronted with anxiety about their creativity, they are at the most fragile point of their working lives. Try to write freely, without critiquing your own work. Don't judge what you are doing, just let it fly from your pen or guitar.

EXERCISES, RHYMING DICTIONARIES, USING A THESAURUS

It's at times like these that you can refer to the various songwriting books that contain exercises. Sheila Davis has written a number of these books, such as *The Songwriter's Idea Book*. In this book she outlines all sorts of plot strategies, such as relationships between children and parents. This may seem like an uninspired way of approaching a creative act, but right now you are seeking any port in a storm.

A number of writers like to use songwriting dictionaries, or a thesaurus, which has words that are similar to, or opposite to, other words. My own experience is that songwriting dictionaries can be of some assistance if I am really stuck, but I prefer not to use them very much. There is something   dictionary rhymes that seems very canned and unspontaneous.

OTHER LYRIC-WRITING EXERCISES

Here is a list of possible song subjects if you are experiencing the dreaded writer's block.

Current events This might be an election, a mine explosion, a war, a heroic act, etc.

Historical events Try writing about something that happened long ago. You may or may not want to use that event as a metaphor for a contemporary happening.

Humorous song Write about something silly in your own life or something that happened to someone that you know.

Friends and family If you rarely write about personal things, try it.

Protest songs Many writers shy away from writing about politics. Certainly in today's complex world there are plenty of things to be concerned about. Try writing about them.

Exotica Write about someplace you've always wanted to visit, but never have. Look at photographs of the place, and even read some books about it.

Breaking the Rules A number of books suggest that you should never write negative songs. Write one

anyway. Write about something or someone you don't like. Try writing it in the first person, as though you are that person, or the third, "he, she," person.

Life-Changing Experiences Construct a song around an experience that you or a friend has had that has profoundly changed your life. If you can't think of such an experience, write it about a character's life in a novel, movie or newspaper story.

Finally, go back to our description of song types in Chapter 3. Try writing one song in a style that is totally new to you.

MELODY-WRITING EXERCISES

Different rhythms If you normally write beautiful ballad melodies, try writing melodies where the rhythmic groove is the centerpiece of the song. If you are more comfortable with upbeat melodies, try to write more thoughtful, darker ones.

Buy a new instrument Buy a new guitar or keyboard. My own experience is that when you pick up an interesting instrument, it will almost begin to write melodies on its own. There are twelve-string guitars, nylon-string guitars, electric rock and jazz guitars and resonator guitars. All of these instruments have different sounds and different capabilities. The same holds true of the many kinds of keyboards that are currently available. Obviously it is not possible to buy dozens and dozens of instruments, and this strategy is probably best saved for when you find yourself in a situation where you feel you are at the end of your melodic rope.

Learn to play a different instrument If you are a piano player, try guitar. If you are a guitar player, try piano, bass or drums. Try to write songs that reflect the strengths of these instruments, rather than recapturing the same style you use in your piano playing on guitar.

GOAL SETTING

It is a good idea to periodically set career goals for yourself. You can structure these goals in terms of creativity or business, or you can set targets in both areas. Useful creative goals might be to develop production skills for demos, learning how to play new (to you) musical styles or instruments, writing songs in new genres, or finding new collaborators.

Business goals might be more along the lines of developing a set of new collaborators, contacting or recontacting music publishers, organizing your songs in a more orderly set of files and demos, and developing contacts with artists, producers or performing rights organizations.

Make a list of things that you want to do, and look at it every three months or so. Often you will find that you are making more progress in your career than you think. On a day-to-day basis it is easy to get caught up in the logistics of a specific song or business deal, and you may not see how far along your career has developed in a period of months or years.

At the same time, it is important to recognize your short-comings or failures. If you persistently find that you are not meeting the goals that you have set, it is time to take an honest look at what you are doing. It is possible that you are choosing the wrong people to associate with, or you may simply be going through a streak of bad luck. On the other hand, you may decide that although songwriting is an enjoyable hobby, it is not a practical career choice for you.

LISTENING TO OTHERS

One final possibility is to listen to other writers who inspire you. Try not to settle on a single writer, or you may find yourself imitating their work. Besides checking out other writers, listen to other musical styles. Even if you don't normally like a specific form of music, whether it be country or rap or you simply don't know about it, studying a new style may provide a new impetus for your songwriting abilities. There is great music being written and performed all over the world, especially in terms of rhythmic vitality and variations, so listen to bossa nova, African music, Eastern European music, and all of the other music that is now readily available to you.

CHAPTER 10 RESOURCES

Davis, Sheila, *The Songwriter's Idea Book,* New York: Writer's Digest, 1992. A good source of ideas for lyrics.

Steve Gillete, *Songwriting and The Creative Process: Suggestions and Starting Points for Songwriters,"* Bethlehem: Sing Out! 1995.

Many writers find it valuable to read novels as a source of inspiration.

Instrumental Music: The Piano

Instrumental music is relatively rare on the pop charts. There are a few artists who are consistent hitmakers, like Kenny G, but for the most part instrumental music is consigned to easy-listening environments, where it becomes background music. New Age music is a sort of hypnotic and repetitious idiom that is primarily an instrumental style. Instrumental music is the dominant style of jazz, and there is a definite if somewhat limited market for it. There are also country and folk musicians who are primarily or entirely instrumental artists, such as Chet Atkins, Bela Fleck or Mark O'Connor. Mark has also crossed over into classical music, performing with cellist Yo-Yo Ma and bassist Edgar Meyer as well as with symphony orchestras. In addition to his renowned bluegrass-and-beyond musical experimentations, Bela has collaborated and recorded with African and Indian musicians.

Beyond the world of records, instrumental music is a key part of film scores, and a large number of radio and television commercials feature instrumental music. So the market for instrumental music is broader than meets the eye at first glance.

Although instrumentalists can be anything from oboists to percussionists, guitar and piano remain the most common instruments. They are also easily the two most popular instruments found in any sort of pop music, and the most accessible instruments on which it is possible to play chords. Even instrumental music that features other instruments usually includes either a piano, a guitar or both.

READING MUSIC

In the appendix of this book is a short section that will enable you to read music, if you don't already have this skill. For now the book will use piano diagrams and guitar tablature. Both of these systems enable musicians to play music without the use of notation. The "piano tablature" is a bit clumsier than the tablature used for guitar, because the piano version doesn't include any kind of rhythmic notation.

This book is intended to help you to develop your skills. Consequently, I haven't made any assumptions about whether or not you can read music. In my judgment reading music is a useful skill that is a handy way to communicate with other musicians, especially if you are involved in music that includes instruments beyond the normal rhythm section. String, horn, and woodwind players normally read music because they are involved in orchestras or ensembles that necessarily use music notation. I know plenty of musicians, good and bad, who read music, and the same thing applies to those who don't read. The bottom line is whether a musician can play, not whether he or she can read music.

Let's turn to the piano and discuss instrumental styles on keyboard instruments.

◆ THE PIANO

There are a number of kinds of pianos, not to mention organs and synthesizers, that are currently available. The grand piano is the monster that is generally found on the concert stage when a pianist plays with the symphony or in a solo recital. The baby grand is a smaller version of that beast, a bit more suitable for living rooms. Upright pianos are long and narrow, and there are thousands of them that were made in the early part of the twentieth century. The spinet is a smaller version of the upright, more suitable to a small house with a limited space.

The length of the piano strings and the size of the soundboard are the factors that make the grand piano so loud and rich in comparison to its smaller companions.

Recently piano makers have come up with digital pianos that have the weighted keys that pianists are used to, but are almost synthesizers, with built-in recording capabilities and memory. There are also modern versions of player pianos that accept discs that enable you to play along with someone else's performances.

Synthesizers are electronic keyboards that contain all sorts of built-in sounds, like imitations of drums, string instruments and horns, and electronic features that are more like what the listener expects to hear played by rock 'n' roll guitarists.

To the right is a very simple piano melody, intended to be played with the right hand alone.

PIANO FIGURE 1

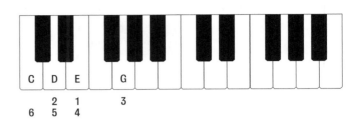

Take the same melody and add chords played with the left hand. These chords are held. In the second bar of the music the chord is played twice, because the chord changes in the bar.

PIANO FIGURE 2

Using the same figure with the right hand; play a chord on all four beats of each bar.

PIANO FIGURE 3

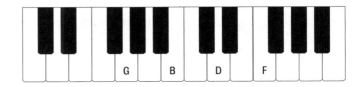

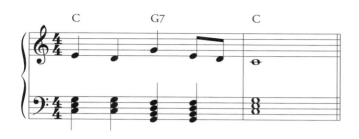

The fourth example will break the chord in the left hand down into arpeggios, or notes of the chord played individually rather than all at once. This is less of a rhythmic sound and more what you might hear being played on a child's music box.

PIANO FIGURE 4

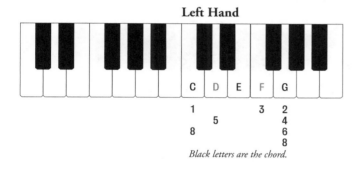

Black letters are the chord.

◆ CHORD INVERSIONS

The notes of the C chord are CEG. It is also possible to invert the chord. Instead of playing CEG, play EGC.

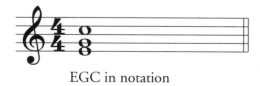

EGC in notation

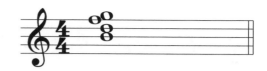

Now let's go back to the same tune with the right hand, but play the arpeggios with the notes EGC for the C chord, and BDFG for the G7 chord.

PIANO EXAMPLE 5

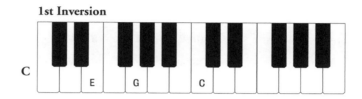

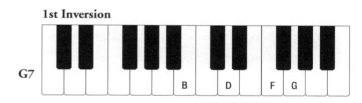

This is called the first inversion of the chord. This simply means that you have started with the second note of the chord.

Now play the C chord GCE, and the G7 chord with the notes DFGB.

PIANO EXAMPLE 6

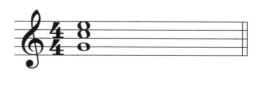

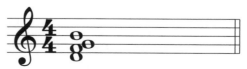

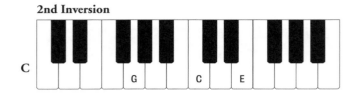

2nd Inversion

C   G   C   E

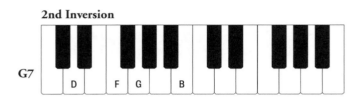

2nd Inversion

G7   D   F   G   B

This is called the second inversion of the chord.

Since the G7 chord has four notes in it, it has a third inversion, which is spelled FGBD.

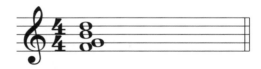

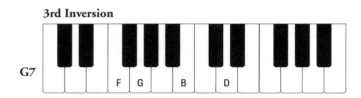

3rd Inversion

G7   F   G   B   D

This is called the third inversion of the chord.

THE PURPOSE OF INVERSIONS

The purpose of playing inversions is to provide some relief from the constant repetition of the same figures. Your ear is the best judge of whether inversions work with any particular tune.

Inversions are very simple to play on the piano, but more difficult for guitarists. If you are playing regularly with a guitarist, be sure that you are not making their life impossible by constantly using inversions. If the piano plays inversions but the guitar omits them, there is a slightly discordant sense in what the listener hears. It isn't the same as playing the "wrong" chord, but it can be an unpleasant sound with repetition.

THE LEFT HAND

Although the left hand rarely plays the melody, by adding and subtracting notes in chords, setting up specific figures like blues or boogie-woogie bass lines, or substituting chords to alter the original harmonic structure of a song you can provide the color to make your melodies more attractive. It can also enable you to hear more complex melodic lines. Below are a few examples.

26 SUSPENSIONS— The Suspended Fourth

To play the suspended fourth you raise the third or middle note of a chord a half tone. CEG becomes CFG. Sooner or later it will resolve back to the original C chord.

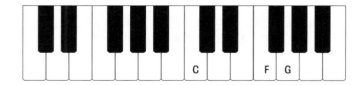

C   F   G

SUSPENDED SECONDS

The suspended second replaces the E note in the C chord with a D. CEG becomes CDG. It too resolves to the original chord (CEG)

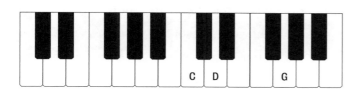

Below is a boogie-woogie bass line. Try inventing your own melody over this bass line, recorded on the CD.

◈ 27 "B o o g i e - W o o g i e"

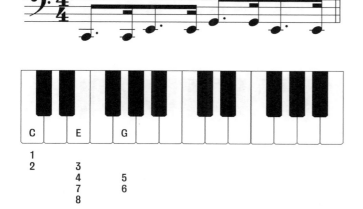

Note that on the CD I improvised some melodic figures that are not written out here. This is simply intended to give you some idea of what the melody could sound like.

CHORDS WITHOUT THIRDS

If you remove the third, or middle note, of a chord you get a kind of hollow, almost medieval sound. Instead of CEG in the left hand, play CG.

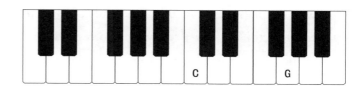

Try the piece below, "Hollow Ground," playing the fifths indicated in the left hand instead of chords.

◈ 28 "H o l l o w   G r o u n d"

"Hollow Ground" with Fifths

"Hollow Ground" with Chords

So that you hear the difference, play the same piece playing the chords indicated with the thirds included in the chords. Notice how different this sounds, even though the melody remains the same.

NEW AGE MUSIC

New Age music is a repetitive, contemplative genre that features languid, sustained chords and wistful melodies. New Age music is used for meditation and for easy listening, and is one form of background music that doesn't necessarily require a high degree of concentrated listening. In other words, it can be used in a dentist's office, or while doing the dishes or just relaxing.

Below is a simple melody in this style, called "Medium Age." For the left hand, simply play the chords in the diagrams. Wherever a chord change appears, play the chord and hold it throughout the bar of music.

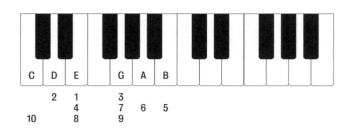

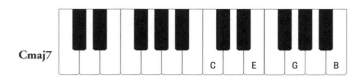

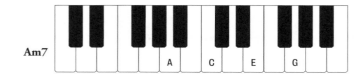

Now try the same piece with the different set of chords indicated in the diagrams. The chords in the second version either go with the melody notes or share common tones with the original chords. For example, C major7 has the notes CEGB, while A minor7 has the notes ACEG. Three of the notes appear in both chords. Your ear is the ultimate judge of whether chord substitutions work. If you substitute a great many chords in a piece, you may lose the effect of the original melody. Depending on how you are using a piece of music, this can be either a good or a poor idea. In a movie score it may provide a way of elaborating on a theme without obviously repeating it.

Substitute Chords

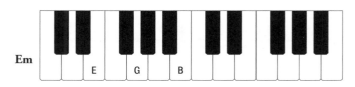

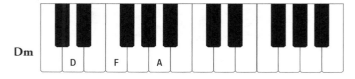

◆29 "Medium Age"

"Medium Age," Chord Substitutes

PEDAL POINTS

A pedal point is a constant tone in the bass that stays the same even though the chords are actually changing. Pedal points give a feeling of uncertainty because the ear loses contact with the harmony of a piece. They are often used in movie scores where the director wants to imply rather than state something that will happen in the film. Sophisticated pop music composers like Jimmy Webb or Burt Bacharach like to use pedal points to disguise or add color to the harmony of a tune. Below is an example of a right-hand melody with a left-hand pedal point droning against it.

㉚ MANY PEDALS

MANY PEDALS VERSION 1

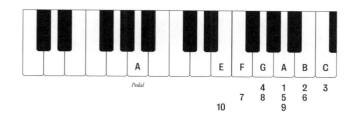

Now try the exact same melody, but play the E in the bass twice, once as written, the next time playing the octave below.

MANY PEDALS VERSION 2

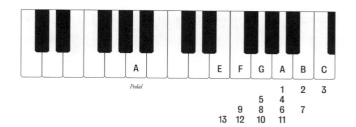

Try the same tune, but elaborate on the melody in the right hand while fooling around with the pedal point rhythms in the left hand. This isn't written out here, but you can hear it on the CD.

㉚ Many Pedals Version 1

Many Pedals Version 2

TECHNOLOGY AND KEYBOARDS: Sequencers, Samplers, Drum Machines and Midi

For relatively little money it is possible to buy keyboard synthesizers that contain MIDI, drum machines and built-in musical samples of other instruments. MIDI stands for Musical Instrument Digital Interface. It enables you to play multiple parts on a keyboard, with computers and other electronic devices sending data to one another. By using a sequencer, musical phrases can be added, subtracted or replicated. It is possible through sequencing to turn a simple figure into a complete rhythm track. Drum machines create similar rhythmic patterns that can be triggered through a synthesizer or by manually manipulating electronic drum pads.

Samplers store various instrumental sounds that can make a keyboard, with overdubbing, sound like a complete orchestral sound palette. Keyboards that contain all of these elements in one keyboard are referred to as "workstations."

CHAPTER 11 RESOURCES

There are dozens of books that can teach you various aspects of playing the piano.

Check out Blake Neely's *Piano for Dummies,* published by IMG books in 1998.

The Rooksby book cited earlier is also a good resource. Hal Leonard Corporation has numerous books for piano. If you are interested in improvising in a wide variety of musical styles, check out Dick Weissman and Dan Fox's book, *A Guide to Non-Jazz Improvisation,* Piano edition, published by Mel Bay in 2009.

At some point you may also want to take private piano lessons.

Technology and the Songwriter

The technology we call MIDI was created to allow musical instruments to communicate with one another via their internal computers. Through MIDI, instruments can talk to each other or to personal computers that run music applications. In addition, computers can talk to one another. This technology—combined with the advent of digital audio recording—has opened up opportunities for songwriters that were previously unknown, but has also created an expectation from the industry that songwriters be tech-savvy.

MIDI AND THE SONGWRITER

Several applications of MIDI technology are particularly useful to musicians and songwriters. Performing musicians can use it to control several synthesizers or sound modules from one controlling keyboard. A sound module is a synth without a keyboard. This is a useful tool for quickly accessing several different sounds in a live performance situation.

SONGWRITING AND SEQUENCERS

The most useful application of MIDI is probably the process called "sequencing." This technology allows songwriters to make arrangements of their songs, audition sounds,

develop beats and create inexpensive demos. There are several different kinds of sequencers, from stand-alone hardware sequencers to applications for personal computers. The most basic one is a drum machine that allows you to create drum parts that can be played back on demand. The sounds the sequencer accesses from the drum machine are often created by digitally recording samples of real instruments or sounds. Drum machines have stored drum sounds that can be accessed by the sequencer within the device. The sequencer tells the machine when to play certain sounds, depending on the order in which they were originally played. This order is stored in the sequencer's memory.

Sequencers don't record sound the way a tape recorder or digital recorder would. They record a performance, which is played back on the instrument by the sequencer as it accesses the stored sounds. It is kind of like a player piano. Piano rolls represent an actual performance, which the player piano punched out on a roll of heavy paper. The roll becomes a record of the original performance, and it can then be put on any player piano. The new piano is the source of the sound for a performance that was recorded on a different piano. The sequencer works in a similar way by remembering what the performer physically did on the keyboard or other input device and recalling and repeating that performance. In fact, many sequencing applications use the term "piano roll" to refer to a way of viewing the performance on the computer screen.

The drum machine has a very basic sequencing capability because it has a limited number of internal sounds and a limited input controller. Most drum machines have buttons or pads for playing or inputting a performance into the sequencer using the different internal sounds. The number of sounds available is relatively limited. This differs from synthesizer keyboards, which have a chromatic keyboard (one with all the notes in any scale) and hundreds of possible sounds. By using MIDI the drum machine's sequencer may be able to access the sounds in a synthesizer, but the limited input capability of the drum machine allows only a few pitches to be played. By utilizing MIDI the synthesizer keyboard can access the drum machine's sounds, as well as those of other synthesizer keyboards and sound modules. It has a full range of chromatic pitches available. This makes the chromatic keyboard a much better choice for an input controller than the drum machine. It should be noted that there are systems for using guitar as an input controller, and there are breath controllers as well, but keyboard is by far the most common way to enter MIDI information into a sequencer.

Many synthesizers also have internal sequencers. (Note that synthesizers are often referred to as keyboards.) The basic ingredients required for sequencing are a chromatic keyboard for note entry, an internal sequencer for storage of performances and internal sounds. Such a keyboard is called a "workstation." Workstations are popular with many songwriters because of their convenience and affordability. However, they have some drawbacks and limitations.

Synthesizers, whether they are keyboards or sound modules, can play only a limited number of notes at a time. This is called the synthesizer's "polyphony." Improvements in memory capacity have allowed this number to exceed 64 notes in most synthesizers. Seldom will a sequence call upon 64 notes at one time, but if you exceed the polyphony of the workstation, notes will not sound. This is why songwriters and studios in the past often had several keyboards and sound modules at their disposal. Working this way is cumbersome and takes up a lot of space. Today, most songwriters who are creating complex sequences use computer-based sequencing applications where all the modules, or plug-ins, as they are called, are in the computer or the application itself.

Workstations often have great sounding internal effects such as reverb, delay or chorus, but may allow only one or two effects to be used at a time. If you have recorded a number of sequenced tracks of different instruments, you may want different effects on each track. Many workstations will not permit this. Here again, you're left with either using a number of sound modules in your sequencing set-up or considering the flexibility of a computer-based workstation. In sequencing applications that are computer based you can use as many different effects or different instances of the same effect that your computer memory will allow.

The decision between using a keyboard workstation or a computer-based sequencing application comes down to what you want to do with it. If you want to make simple demos and use sequencing primarily to audition arrangements, create beats or sketch ideas, the keyboard workstation would probably work well. It is compact and less expensive than an investment in a computer-based system. However, if you want to create professional demos and more complex arrangements you will probably find the keyboard workstation inadequate. Applications for the personal computer are much more flexible and easier to navigate. Also, most sequencing applications for personal computer also allow for digital audio recording, something that keyboard workstations don't do.

THE ADVANTAGES OF MIDI

Sequencers are equipped with a "clock" which drives the sequencer and keeps the tempo steady. With MIDI any one sequencer can drive the clock of another. A drum machine can be the master and drive a workstation and personal computer application, or the computer application can be the master and drive a rack of sound modules while also playing internal plug-in modules within the application. There are many possible configurations. One of the great advantages of MIDI sequencing is that it gives you the ability to change the instrument or sound used for a performance after the performance has been recorded. We can change the sound at any time by assigning the performance to a new plug-in, sound module or synthesizer.

Imagine that you recorded a performance into a workstation using an internal piano sound, and then decided that you would have preferred an organ sound. We can bring a friend's synthesizer that has that sound, hook it up via MIDI to our keyboard, play the sequence, and assign the part to his organ sound. Our original piano performance is now an organ track.

If our friend leaves and takes his synth, however, we no longer have the organ sound available. This is why studios may utilize several sound modules, or more often, have gone to computer-based applications where they can have sound module plug-ins with thousands of sounds at their disposal. The only other option we have is to digitally record the organ sound before the friend leaves. Unfortunately, there could be no further editing of the performance after this.

A songwriter can use a single keyboard with an internal sequencer or he might connect a keyboard synthesizer as an input controller, and possibly other sound modules or a drum machine, to a personal computer that can run a music sequencing application. With internal sound bank plug-ins, this is certainly sufficient to create a nice MIDI studio. Plug-in modules function virtually just like hardware sound modules or synths. Each is capable of receiving MIDI information on at least sixteen different channels. A personal computer sequencer can speak to several different MIDI instruments internally or externally if connected via a MIDI interface. This allows dozens of tracks to play simultaneously, depending on the number of instruments connected via the MIDI interface and the number of internal plug-in modules.

MIDI TRACKS

MIDI tracks also utilize dynamics, duration and other parameters. Sounds stored in a keyboard or sound module are often called "programs." A sequencer can transmit a program change to change a sound in the middle of a track. Pitch bends, volume changes, velocity (how hard a key is struck) and changes of key (modulation) can also be transmitted. These can be recorded during the initial performance or changed later. You can also change where the notes occur and the velocity. You can also cut and paste as you can in word processing programs. You might record two bars of a bass line and copy them four times to get eight bars. Wrong notes can be edited out and new notes added. These editing possibilities are extremely useful, especially if your keyboard skills are limited. Of course, you change the tempo, too, recording a track slowly them speeding it up to the tempo you want.

The human voice cannot yet be sequenced. Songs still require a singer. Although, sampling technology is improving all the time, some instruments are still not convincing when sequenced. Keyboard instruments simply cannot emulate the performance of instrumentalists on some instruments. With careful editing, however, most instruments can be emulated or imitated with reasonable success.

Sometimes it is more aesthetically pleasing to use a real

instrument and a live musician on a demo. When a live performer is used, the singer for example, their performance must be recorded as an audio track that is synchronized with the sequenced tracks. The easiest way to accomplish this is with a computer application that combines sequencing and digital audio recording technologies. A live performer can be combined with many pre-recorded sequenced tracks that were created through the use of MIDI. The biggest problem is carefully keeping track of everything you have recorded.

DIGITAL AUDIO RECORDING

The ability to digitally record audio directly to a computer has opened up a new world for home recording. There are two types of digital recorders. One is the stand-alone unit with an internal computer and storage drive that is dedicated to sound recording only. These units can record from eight to thirty-two tracks or more, depending on how elaborate a setup you can afford. They can also be synchronized to a sequencer via MIDI so that you can listen to sequenced tracks and record live along with them.

There are also a number of hand-held recorders of the stand-alone type available to the songwriter. These very portable devices can be quite sophisticated, with built-in microphones and the capability to record up to four tracks at once at CD quality or better. Some specialize in recording two tracks at once but have the capability for multi-track recording up to four tracks. Some are equipped with external mic inputs. The sound files can be dumped into a personal computer and imported into a digital audio application for editing or further multi-track recording. These can be a valuable tool for the songwriter for sketching ideas and recording rehearsals and live performances.

The second type of digital audio recorder is found in the digital audio applications designed for use on the personal computer. These applications digitally record music directly onto the computer's hard disk or an external drive. Most digital recording applications combine the MIDI sequencing and recording functions in one program, allowing for easy synchronization of the two technologies.

The digital recording of sound to disk is the same technology that creates CDs and samples of sound. Hard disk recorders record tracks of sound at a rate equal to or better than that used to make CDs. The sample rate for CDs is 44.1kHz, and it requires about 600 to 700 megabytes of memory to store a single hour of stereo sound recorded at this rate. You can see that multi-track digital audio recording requires considerable memory.

Recording sound to disk is also hard on the formatting of the disk. Don't use a hard drive that has other applications and files stored on it. When recording audio, the recording application will place pieces of the recording wherever it can find space on the disk. This can endanger other materials stored on the disk. It can also affect the integrity of the audio file if it is too fragmented. Use a drive that is dedicated only to the storage of sound files and related materials. The drive must also have an access time that is fast enough to keep up with the recording application. Not all external hard drives meet this application. Many people prefer the use of FireWire or USB for this reason.

A home studio that has MIDI sequencing and digital audio recording technologies in place can effectively produce multi-track recordings with the sort of complexity used in an acoustic orchestral arrangement. All of the sequenced and digitally recorded tracks can be mixed via a mixing board to a stereo master. This can all be accomplished within the application if no external sound sources are used. The master can be recorded and exported as a sound file, burned to a CD or recorded to analog or digital tape externally. This technology is ubiquitous in our society today.

One example of how this technology has become so common and available is the Macintosh application Garage Band. Mac includes this application as a standard feature with most of their new computers. Garage Band is a fully functional sequencer and multi-track, digital audio recorder with an included bank of sounds, beats, loops and effects. Although you probably wouldn't use this application to record a CD, it is capable of creating very effective and professional sounding demos. There are also some freeware and shareware applications available on the internet for download which provide multi-track, digital audio recording capabilities.

Song demos can be successfully created in home studios with these technologies. It is even quite common to see commercially successful recordings that have been produced with modest equipment in home studios. A home studio may not have all of the expensive gear that a professional operation possesses, but the home studio engineer can invest as much time as she wishes to get a successful result.

MUSIC NOTATION APPLICATIONS

Technology has now given us the ability to use MIDI functions and computer applications that can mechanically notate music. These applications provide easy entry of notes into a score or guitar tablature, and don't require the composer to physically write out the music. By using a laser printer, the quality is as good as that of any professional publisher. Many of the examples in this book were created using a personal computer, music notation application and a laser printer. Notes can be entered by using a keyboard connected via a MIDI interface to a personal computer running the notation application. This is the same setup we looked at when discussing MIDI sequencing with the personal computer. The notes can be played into the score in real time by playing to a metronome beat, or they can

be entered in step-time, one note or chord at a time.

Notation applications contain a sequencer and many sequencer applications have notation capability. Each does its primary function best, but they are based on the same technology. Many functions of the notation application are similar to those of a sequencing application. These include quantization (time correction) and automotive duration adjustment, for notes that are not held down for the proper duration.

There are numerous other tools for the correcting and formatting of scores. Because the notation application is basically a sequencer with notation as an emphasis, it is possible to print out a MIDI file as a score. There is usually some amount of formatting and adjustment required to attain a readable score, but the note entry part will be completed in the original sequencing process.

It is also possible to translate a score into a MIDI file. The notation application will usually have playback capability, but it is not as sophisticated as a dedicated sequencer. By exporting the MIDI file from the notation application and importing it into a sequencing application, it can be manipulated and played back with greater sophistication than the playback capability found within the notation application itself. Many composers working in film and television write their scores in a notation application and export the MIDI file into a sequencing application for a final mock-up. It may be a draft for a feature film, which will later be recorded by an orchestra, or it might be a final arrangement to be mastered for the film or television production.

TECHNOLOGY AND THE SONGWRITER

Many songwriters can and do utilize the technologies discussed in this chapter. These technologies can be used with whatever level of sophistication and complexity the writer's skills and tastes allow. Technology, however, is still a tool to be utilized by humans, not a device intended to enslave them. In other words, a performance of a song must convey emotion. The technology should aid and abet the creative process and not replace it.

Doug Krause, Senior Instructor
University of Colorado Denver

CHAPTER 12 RESOURCES

Since technology is constantly changing, we suggest that you consult the latest catalog or website of Hal Leonard Corporation to check out the latest resources available about MIDI, sequencing, samplers, etc.

Songwriting and Melody Writing with the Guitar

TYPES OF GUITARS

The guitar is a wonderful vehicle for songwriting. It can be played in many different styles, and the instrument itself is made from different kinds of woods, and comes in a variety of sizes. If the guitar isn't portable enough for you, it is now possible to purchase travel guitars that are not much larger than ukuleles and actually have a pretty decent sound. (The bad news is that the good ones aren't cheap.)

Although this is a bit of an over-simplification, guitarists break down into two basic groups: those who play with their fingers and those who play with a pick. Each playing style has its advantages and disadvantages. Playing with a pick enables you to play at lightning-fast speed, and it also makes it possible to play heavy rhythm guitar without any fear of damaging your fingernails.

The disadvantage of pick playing is that you can't play more than one string at a time, unless you have mastered playing with both a pick and your fingers. This is, unfortunately, one of the more difficult right-hand techniques.

Playing with your fingers enables you to use more dynamics. It's easier to play softer, and to vary the volume of your

bass notes in relation to the treble notes, and vice versa. You will also be able to play complete chords, with all the notes sounding at once rather than consecutively. The classical guitar is wonderfully suited for softer and more melodic playing, and the flamenco guitar, made of cypress wood, allows for tremendous power.

Then there is the electric guitar. With an electric guitar and a quality amplifier it is possible to get all sorts of wild and unusual sounds. Electrics can also produce much more sustain than acoustic guitars.

To further confuse matters there are f-hole guitars, acoustic guitars with violin-like f-holes instead of a round center sound hole. These guitars have a unique and wonderful sound especially suited for jazz. Freddie Greene, who played for many years with the late Count Basie, could practically propel the whole band with his rhythmic playing on an f-hole model.

It is possible to get very different sounds on the guitar depending on the number of strings you choose to play, and whether the strings are open or stopped. An open-string chord means that some of the strings are not fingered by the left hand; these strings ring out more than ones that are fretted. For country and folk styles, open-string chords are considered very desirable. The musical fragment below uses many open strings

31 "Wide Open"

"WIDE OPEN" Version #2

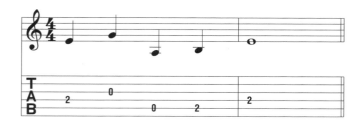

Try the same piece, but add the sixth string played by the right thumb without any left-hand fingering. This note is played on the first note of each bar.

"WIDE OPEN" Version #2

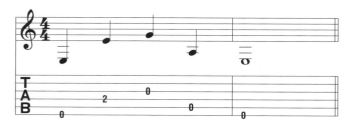

Let's take some time to go over a few right-hand techniques. All of them are played on the CD.

THUMB ALONE

This is probably the simplest way of playing the guitar. Simply strum across the strings of the guitar with your thumb. Try an E minor chord. In this simple technique you are using the right thumb as though it were a pick.

32 THUMB AND INDEX FINGER

Stay with the E minor chord. Play a bass note, say the sixth string and the fourth string, alternating. With your index finger brush down across the strings. The two notes are even quarter notes. What you have now is:

1) Thumb plays sixth string or fourth string
2) Index finger brushes down across three or four strings

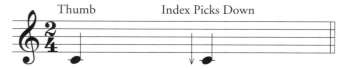

DOUBLING THE INDEX

This strum is the same as the one above, except that now the index finger brushes back up as well as down. The rhythm is a quarter note, followed by two eighth notes, or long, short, short.

33 Bass Rumble

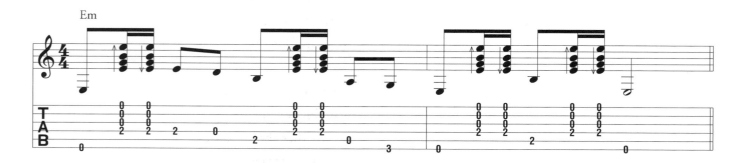

1) Thumb plays sixth or fourth string.

2) Index finger brushes down across strings.

3) Index finger brushes back up across strings.

Try the piece, "Bass Rumble," on page 92 which demonstrates the third strum with an E minor chord adding a few notes not in the chord, as diagrammed.

BASS RUMBLE

The right-hand position for this strum, sometimes called the Carter Family strum, after Maybelle Carter, a pioneering country guitarist, is either resting your ring finger on the wood of the guitar or holding your wrist free.

❖34 THE ARPEGGIO

The arpeggio is one of the most important techniques used in classical guitar. Think of your right thumb as the custodian of the bass strings—the sixth, fifth and fourth strings. Your index finger plays the third string, the middle finger plays the second string, and the ring finger plays the first string. Stay with the E minor chord for now.

On the CD you will hear the arpeggio played in two ways:

Arpeggio #1
1) Thumb plays sixth or fourth string

2) Index finger plays the third string, while the middle finger plays the second string and the ring finger plays the first string.

Both parts of this pattern are even quarter notes.

Now try the same pattern, except that you will play all of the strings separately.

1) Thumb plays sixth or fourth string.

2) Index finger plays the third string.

3) Middle finger plays the second string.

4) Ring finger plays the first string.

The rhythm is four even eighth notes.

In arpeggio playing you hold the right hand in an arched position over the sound hole of the guitar. Only the thumb picks downward; the other fingers pick up, or toward your body. The object of the strum is for each note to be crystal clear.

❖35 TRAVIS PICKING (FINGERPICKING)

Travis picking is named after legendary country picker Merle Travis. It is also known as fingerpicking. In the basic pattern the right thumb alternates with the index and middle fingers.

Playing the E minor chord again the simplest pattern is:

1) Thumb plays sixth string (pick down).

2) Middle finger plays first string (pick up).

3) Thumb plays fourth or third string (pick down).

4) Index finger plays second string (pick up).

The notes are eighth notes. For the moment play them evenly.

The right-hand position that most players use is resting the ring finger of the right hand against the wood near the sound hole. Some players use the index finger for both notes, ignoring the middle finger.

Below are a few Travis-style variations, followed by an original piece based on this style.

Travis Pick #2

1) Thumb plays sixth string.

2) Thumb plays fourth string while middle finger plays first string.

3) Index finger plays second string.

4) Thumb plays sixth string.

5) Middle finger plays first string.

6) Thumb plays fourth or third string.

7) Index finger plays second string.

The rhythm is a quarter note followed by six eighth notes.

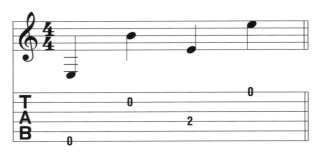

Travis Pick #3

This strum is similar to the first one, but with the index and middle fingers playing in reverse order:

1) Thumb plays sixth string.

2) Index finger plays second or third string.

3) Thumb plays fourth string.

4) Middle finger plays first string.

The following piece is based on Travis picking but also contains extra notes that are not in the strum. If you are interested in writing pieces in this style, it is important to be able to move in and out of the patterns. Melodies rarely fit perfectly into specific right-hand picking patterns. In the same way there are notes added outside the chords. Notice that I have played this short piece twice. The repeat is not written out, but is an improvisation based on the tune. I'll have more to say about this later in the chapter.

36 Travising Light

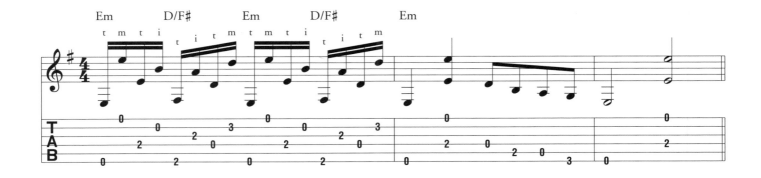

◆37◆ LATIN AMERICAN STYLES

There are quite a few interesting Mexican and South American guitar styles. Try the rhythm pattern below and see if any melodies emerge from the chords. Try it with the ordinary chords, then with the barre chords covering all six strings. If you are not used to playing barre chords, you may find it difficult to get a good sound out of them.

There are eight steps to this strum:

1) Brush down with three or four fingers on the guitar, and immediately deaden the strings with the palm of your hand.

2) While the strings are deadened, hit the strings and the wood of the guitar by releasing the left-hand fingers off the chord.

3) Brush up as in one, deaden the strings with your left hand.

4) Brush down across the string.

5) Bush back across strings.

6) Brush down across strings.

7) Brush back across strings.

Deadening the strings is actually part of the rhythm, so the feeling is a quarter note followed by six eighth notes.

There isn't room in this book to go into tremendous detail about guitar strums, but experiment with playing bossa nova and reggae strums with your fingers.

PICK-STYLE GUITAR

The flat pick is usually held between the thumb and first finger of the right hand. The sound that you get will be affected by the thickness and hardness of the pick. Really thin picks tend to make more noise as they brush across the strings. You have to decide for yourself what sort of picks you like. Most guitar players carry different kinds of picks in order to get different sounds.

You can use the pick in the same way that you tried the Carter family strums. Use the E minor chord. The rhythm is quarter note, eighth, eighth.

◆38◆ "Greene Scene"

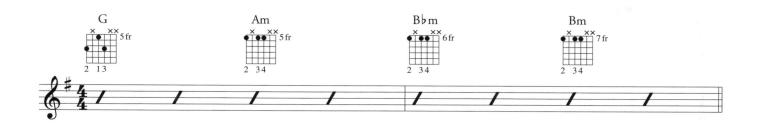

1) Pick down on sixth or fourth string.

2) Pick down across top three or four strings.

3) Pick back across top two or three strings.

Try the chunky Freddie Greene jazz guitar rhythm in the following example. Be sure to use the chords as diagrammed, and deaden the strings that are not fingered with the left hand. In the same way that you deadened the strings in the Mexican strum, deaden each chord after you have picked it. Snap the pick with your right wrist to help you get the chunky sound.

THE BLUES

Blues guitar styles range from very basic rhythm strumming to electrifying lead playing, with complex fingerpicking patterns in between. A great deal of the character of blues playing comes from the instrumental fills that occur between the vocals. Try the blues strum below with an E major chord:

1) Thumb plays sixth or fourth string, while the middle finger picks up on the first string.

2) Index finger picks up on the second string.

The rhythm is long, short, or a dotted eight note followed by a sixteenth note. The same strum can be done with the middle finger omitted and the index finger playing all of the upstroked notes. Fills can be played with either the thumb and index finger or the index and middle finger alternating the notes. Try the "Milwaukee Blues" fragment below.

40 TUNINGS AND SLIDE GUITAR

The guitar is usually tuned EADGBE. There are several other tunings that are in wide use, especially among blues players. The G tuning contains the notes DGDGBD, and the D tuning is spelled DADF♯AD. Both of these tunings are "open tunings." This means that if you strum across the strings without any left-hand fingering you will, in the case of the G tuning, play a G chord, and in the D tuning you will play a D chord.

In slide guitar playing you either hold a slide in your left hand or, more commonly, wear it on the ring finger or little finger of your left hand. Be sure that you place the

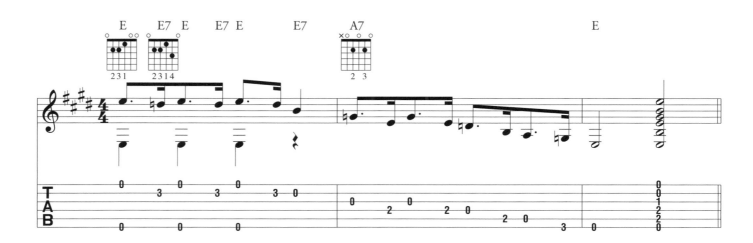

39 "Milwaukee Blues"

slide *over* the frets, and not just behind them, as you do in other styles of playing—the slide is taking the place of the fret. Below are the G, C and D chords, diagrammed in the G tuning.

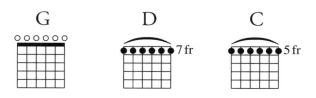

Rather than playing an actual guitar piece, I am going to play G D C G on the guitar. You can see that this style of playing suggests a whole different type of approach to playing the blues, in terms of what the instrument does and where your melody is apt to go.

🔷 41 ROCK GUITAR IMPROV

There are a bewildering number of rock guitar styles. Rhythm and lead guitar, folk rock, country rock, heavy metal, punk and many other styles all can be played on the electric guitar.

Folk rock guitar is sort of juiced-up folk guitar, with some of the figures played on electric guitar. Try alternating the two chords below: D and Am7.

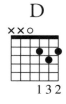
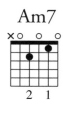

🔷 42 POWER CHORDS

Power chords are chord fragments that are played on two or three strings. They are generally played on the bass

strings with the volume cranked way up. Power chords have a kind of hollow sound, because the middle note of the chord is often omitted. So a C power chord would have the notes C and G, not CEG.

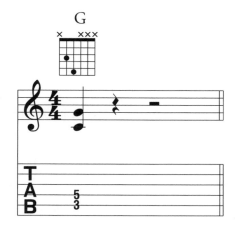

Follow the chord diagrams below, and play "Find the Power." The rhythm is long short, long short, long short, long short, or a dotted eighth note followed by a sixteenth note. Then repeat the whole phrase.

long, short, long, short, etc.

Find the Power

This has only been a brief discussion of rock guitar. There are many techniques to be mastered before you are fluent in this style. They include bending the strings, playing notes with the left hand (hammering on), pulling off notes with the left hand, and tapping, where both hands hammer on the neck simultaneously. By studying some or all of these techniques you should be able to brighten up your instrumental writing and provide ideas for your songwriting as well.

IMPROVISING

Virtually all proficient musicians in popular music have developed their skills at improvisation. Improvisation means that you take a set melodic or chordal figure and make up new parts from it. In the most extreme forms of improvisation you start without any melody at all and simply play spontaneously.

It is important for popular musicians to develop improvisational skills for a number of reasons. Melodies often emerge from especially creative improvisations, and songs that may be relatively simple and obvious develop whole new dimensions of musicality when spiced by inspired improvisations.

Improvisations can emerge from chords, from the melodies themselves or simply out of rhythmic bursts of energy. Listen to the CD for an improvised blues, made up in the recording studio. We have deliberately not notated it here. It is in the key of E.

CHAPTER 13 RESOURCES

There are literally hundreds of instructional books on guitar. A reasonable place to start is *Guitar for Dummies* by Mark Phillips and Jon Chappell, published by IDG books in 1998.

Hal Leonard Corporation and Mel Bay Publications both have numerous books on various styles of guitar and piano. Most people also benefit from taking private lessons.

Jamey Aebersold publishes numerous recordings accompanied by sheet music that can help you develop improvisational skills. If you are interested in improvising music in a broad variety of styles, check out *A Guide to Non-Jazz Style Improvisation Guitar edition*, by Dick Weissman and Dan Fox, published by Mel Bay Publications in 2009.

Putting It All Together: The Song and the Demo

We have now looked in some depth at both lyrics and melodies. Before we move over into the business aspects of songwriting, let's try to put the creative process in perspective. Obviously successful songs must contain both lyrics and melodies. Is one more important than the other? Harriet Schock, writing in her songwriting text *Becoming Remarkable,* states that melodies should come first. It is her belief that a great lyric cannot survive a poor melody, but that "the reverse of this isn't always true." I would modify this point of view by stating that a performance by a particular artist may well succeed in convincing the public that a particular song is worthy of their attention (and dollars). As we move into the twenty-first century I would include the notion that brilliant production may even substitute for the more traditional notion of a performance, or, for that matter, a well-crafted song.

The problem for the songwriter who is not a recording artist is that he or she must convince someone to record the song in the first place. If the artist has no monetary interest in the song—that is, he or she doesn't own any share of the publishing and is not a co-writer—It is a mistake for the songwriter to count on the artist (or producer) to rescue his mediocre song.

COLLABORATION AS THE GLUE TO BIND A SONG

Ideally, collaboration maximizes the strengths of two or more writers, eliminating the weak points in the writers' abilities. (In fact, this may well occur.) Collaboration can also result in a song becoming more limited than it might have in the mind of the writer who dreamed up the original ideas. Let's go back to the idea of collaboration and try to relate it to the notion of completing a song.

How do collaborations evolve? People who work together in bands often collaborate because they spend so much time together, and because they have an outlet for their work. Non-performing writers develop collaborations through music publishers, friends and industry contacts. There are several downsides of collaboration. The most obvious one is that the writers will split the royalties. The artistic drawback may be that the writer who came up with the original idea may find that his vision of the song has been destroyed in the give-and-take of collaboration. It is also true that some people work faster than others, which is not to say that faster equates with better. The slower writer may get steamrollered in the process, and therefore will find that his input into the final song is diminished or even eliminated.

WRITING FOR THE MARKET

There are several dozen books on the market about songwriting. They all mention song hooks, titles, verses, choruses and bridges. Many of them have rules that they feel all writers should follow. One example is the one mentioned earlier in this book, that artists want to see themselves depicted in a positive way, and hesitate to deal with anything that will give them a negative image. Other such "rules" concern the length of songs, stylistic mannerisms of specific genres of music, and the nature of rhymes.

The fundamental question that you have to ask yourself is whom you are writing for, and how important is it to you to be successful. If you are writing strictly for the marketplace, then it is probably best to observe these rules, or at least to be aware of them. If your primary concern is to write to express yourself, then why would you be concerned with formulas? The sticking point, of course, is the problem of making a living. But the news isn't all bad. Following the rules is no guarantee of monetary success. After all, there are hundreds of writers who *are* following the rules, but there aren't hundreds of them who become rich and famous.

Just before I began to write this chapter, I read a book called *The Soul of a Writer: Intimate Interviews With Successful Songwriters,* written by Susan Tucker and Linda Lee Strother. A number of the writers interviewed stated that their greatest success came when they stopped listening to the rule-makers and followed their own hearts and minds.

Keep in mind that many major artists and writers have repeatedly had their work rejected by record companies and music publishers. The business needs new and innovative artists, but by the same token, it tends to be suspicious of music that is not easy to classify.

BEWARE OF THE EDITOR AND THE CRITIC

In the same book there is a considerable amount of attention devoted to writers' over-intellectualizing their own process. The critic is the part of you that takes apart every line that you come up with, feeling that it is stupid or stereotyped. My best friend in college could have, and should have, been a brilliant novelist. Every time he set pen to paper he could scarcely get through completing a line before the rational, critical part of his brain would devastate his own work. Consequently he never pursued creative writing as a profession.

The editor is another part of you. The editor is the part of you that does the rewrites of your songs.

FOR AND AGAINST EDITING

Some years ago I lived next door to an excellent painter. It became a community joke, one that he occasionally shared in, that the best time to look at Herb's paintings was when he had, in effect, done a "first draft." If you waited until he thought the work was finished, you would lose much of the original energy and soul of the work. The work had become too densely layered, and every part of the canvas was filled with information. This detracted from the vitality of the work as it appeared in an earlier stage.

The same thing can happen to songs. If every line is brutally reworked, you may very well have a more perfect final product. But have you retained the original energy and impact of the story you are trying to tell?

I am not maintaining that you shouldn't rewrite your songs. I am saying that there is a point where you have to let the child walk into the world without holding its hand. People generally don't read or recite songs, they sing them. The final test of the song's efficacy is whether anyone wants to sing it, or to hear others perform it. This doesn't mean that you should accept first drafts of your songs as though they were dictated by a higher power. It is a good idea to put new songs aside for a few days. Come back to them and, if possible, put them on tape. Do the lyrics and the music work together? Are there superfluous words that are there only because you wanted to fill in the line? Is the first verse interesting enough that the listener wants to hear the rest of the song? Is the chorus really the strongest part of the song? Is the order of verses coherent, or is it just the order in which you came up with it?

DEMOS

When you have decided that your song is completed, it is time to put together some sort of demo for artists or record producers. I am assuming here that you are not the artist who will be singing the song. If you *are* the artist who will perform the song, then all you really need to do is to make a rough demo so that you will remember the stylistic nuances of the song while it is still fresh in your mind.

Now you must confront what sort of demo you should make. I have read books that maintain that a demo with just a vocal with guitar or piano is sufficient, and others that suggest making a demo produced in the style of the artist that you hope will record the song.

In my opinion the decision should mostly be based on the style of the music and who is going to listen to the demo. Many of the people in the music industry have very little understanding of music but a fine understanding of marketing. To such a listener, pounding your acoustic guitar will still not make your song into a rock tune. If he doesn't hear bass and drums, then in his mind it can't be a rock song.

On the other hand, if the listener is a skilled musician, especially a music arranger, he or she may very well prefer to hear the song in as simple a form as possible, filling in his own ideas about what the song would sound like with a country rhythm section, or a Latin drummer.

The problem is that you may very well be playing your demo for both sorts of industry listeners. There may not be a possible compromise that will be satisfactory for both of these groups. The best solution may be something between the two extremes. A vocal demo, for example, with at least a rhythm section.

If you are planning to enter any sort of songwriting contest, you should be particularly attentive to the quality of your demo. Applications for these contests usually claim that it doesn't make much difference if the demo is well-produced because the people listening are skilled professionals. Put yourself in the shoes of someone listening to hundreds of demos in search of awarding a few songs prizes. Doesn't it stand to reason that you will be more receptive to a demo that features an excellent singer with a tightly rehearsed band? To put it another way, if you yourself question your vocal abilities, don't sing on a demo you submit for a contest.

MAKING THE DEMO

If you do not have a music publisher who is paying for the demo, the goal is to make a good demo but limit your costs. You will have to pay for a studio, musicians and, if you are not a good singer, a singer, or even several singers, if you want background vocals.

How much will you have to pay for a good demo? In the larger cities there are people who specialize in making demos. They are able to come into the studio and very quickly learn the song, and do a creditable job of performing it. This may well turn out to be cheaper than having a friend sing the song who burns up a lot of studio time because she can't quite hit the right notes.

There is also the question of who will produce the demo. You cannot necessarily rely on the engineer at a recording studio to do this for you. You also need to be sure that the performance is proceeding along the lines that you, the writer, have in mind.

There are demo services that offer to produce demos if you send them your own rough demos of a song, or a lead sheet. Some of these production studios are very professional, but personally, I would be reluctant to have someone produce a demo for me if I could not be in the studio to critique the performance and arrangement of the song.

BUDGETS

Many people now own basic recording equipment. The price of purchasing reasonable recording gear has gone way down. Whether you are recording on ADAT formats or on hard disk, it is possible to get a well-produced demo with equipment that previously was available only in studios. But does your friend with the equipment also have high-quality microphones, and outboard gear for getting special effects?

It is also possible to do the basic recording in a home studio and then mix it in a professional studio that has these capabilities. That way you won't have to be biting your nails when the singer takes two hours to complete a project that you budgeted and estimated at thirty minutes.

If you are a good musician or singer, it is also possible to trade off services with other songwriters with skills that differ from yours. You play guitar on their demo, and they sing on yours.

There are a few basic things to remember.

1) Can you understand the lyrics of the song? If not, either you have a singer with bad diction, you have

written a clumsy set of lyrics, or you have mixed the instrumental parts too loud.

2) Avoid long introductions. If you are playing the song for a publisher, an artist or a record producer, they just want to hear the song.

3) For the same reasons as above, avoid long instrumental solos.

4) On the positive side, if you have worked out a catchy guitar or piano figure, include it in your demo. It may very well end up on the finished record, imitated by another musician. Another possibility is that you will end up playing on the session yourself, earning more income as a session player. (Current union rates exceed $300 for a three-hour session.) According to Jason Blume in his book *6 Steps to Songwriting Success,* demo singers in Nashville charge $60 to $75 for country demos, whereas the best studio vocalists in New York and Los Angeles charge as much as $300 a song. Remember that a superior vocal performance is probably the single most important factor in getting results from a demo.

5) On your cassette box, or inside the CD, write your name, address and phone number on the box and on the cassette or CDR itself. You never know when the song might be separated from the tape box, and if the publisher or artist can't find it he won't know how to contact you.

6) Always include lyric sheets. Many people in the popular music business can't read music, so lead sheets aren't really necessary. If you find it easy to write a lead sheet, it's not a bad idea to include it.

7) If you expect the song to be returned to you if it is rejected, include a self-addressed, stamped envelope with it. Don't call the publisher right away; give them several weeks to listen before you call.

8) Some writers include a check sheet that asks the publisher if they can continue to send material, and what material the publisher is looking for.

9) Expect rejection. If you are attempting to pursue a long-term career, you need to learn from rejection. Did you get a form letter, or a personal letter with some suggestions about your work? If the latter is the case, be sure to follow up with the publisher.

10) Another reason to pursue collaboration is that your collaborator may possess useful musical skills that will result in good demos. She may be a fine singer or keyboard player, while you are an adequate background singer but an excellent guitarist. Together you may well be able to provide practically complete demos, without having to hire additional musicians or vocalists.

CHAPTER 14 RESOURCES

Susan Tucker and Linda Lee Strother, *The Soul of a Writer,* published by Journey Publishing Co., Nashville, TN, 1996.

The Money: Sources of Income

WHERE THE MONEY COMES FROM

There are a variety of sources of income that go to the successful songwriter. They are:

1) **Mechanicals** This is income from the sale of records. Currently the rate that record companies pay to music publishers is 9.01 cents for each song on an album, or 1.75 cents per minute of playing time, whichever is larger. This means that if you write long instrumental suites you will be enjoying income at the higher rate. The same royalty is paid for digital downloads of songs.

2) **Performance rights** These are the rights to air songs on radio and television. Public venues such as large restaurants and stadiums also pay performance royalties for the right to have songs performed. Little if any of this money goes directly to songwriters; instead it is paid into the general fund of one of the three performing rights organizations. These organizations are ASCAP, BMI and SESAC. As we will see there are similarities and differences in the ways that they operate.

3) **Synchronization rights** Synchronization, or synch rights, are the rights to use music with pictures. These rights include film and television. The studio or network pays a flat fee for the right to use your music with the picture. There are no set fees for these uses. Commercials are also "leased" in this way.

4) **Print rights** This is the right to print music. A half dozen music publishers control the bulk of this market. These companies mostly lease the rights to print music, and they do not own much in the way of copyrights. Print rights were the major source of income for music publishers in the early part of the twentieth century, and although they are considerably less important now, they can still represent a good source of income for the songwriter and music publisher. Certain songs are often performed at such events as weddings and enjoy strong sheet music sales over a long period of time.

5) **Grand rights** Grand rights are the rights that govern the use of theater music in plays (not, however, in movies), This income is split between the composer, the lyricist and the author of the book for the play. There are usually two or three different people who share this income.

6) **Etc.** Song lyrics may be reprinted in books, magazines, greeting cards, T-shirts, music boxes, etc. All of the fees for these uses are negotiable.

7) **New media rights** These include ringtones and

ringbacks. According to Jeffrey Brabec's and Todd Brabec's book, *Music, Money and Success,* sixth edition, these rates can be flat fees of 10-20 cents for each download of a song or instrumental piece, or 10-12% of the price paid by the consumer.

MECHANICALS

Let's look at more details about these various sources of income. First of all, all income from songs is split 50-50 between the songwriter and the music publisher. All income goes directly to the publisher, who then pays the songwriter. The only exception to this is performance royalty income, which is paid directly to BMI, ASCAP or SESAC. They in turn pay the writer and the publisher separately.

Although there is a set fee for mechanicals, it is quite common for record companies to negotiate for a 3/4 payout. This means that the 9.01 royalty per song is often, in fact, 6.76 cents. There are two way that this usually works.

When the record company also owns the music publishing rights the contract may provide that songs will be licensed at the reduced rate. The other method of enforcing this rate, called a *controlled composition clause,* is that the record company will set a ceiling on what it is willing to pay in mechanicals on a CD. Let's imagine that this rate is 57 cents. What this means is that the record company will not pay more than this, no matter how many songs appear on a CD. If the artist is a songwriter, but only an occasional one, and chooses to do outside songs by major writers, all of the publishing royalties may go to the other writers, and the artist-songwriter may end up with no songwriting income at all from record sales.

To make matters worse, there is another cute device called *cross collateralization.* If the record company owns the publishing on an artist-writer's songs, they may charge that income against the artist's royalties, until the artist has paid off all advances on his album.

If your head is spinning at this point, you might want to consult one of my two books about the music business, *Making a Living in Your Local Music Market,* or *Understanding the Music Business.*

PERFORMANCE ROYALTIES

There are three performing rights organizations. ASCAP is the oldest, dating back to 1914. It is owned by the songwriters and publishers, and is a nonprofit organization. BMI was founded in 1939, and is technically owned by the broadcasters.

Performance rights are negotiated between the performing rights organizations and the radio and television stations. In 1939 ASCAP tried to raise its rates, and the broadcasters responded by starting their own performing rights society. It may appear a bit odd to you that the broadcasters own an organization that they must negotiate with on the setting of rates, but both BMI and ASCAP operate under federal court decrees, and the federal courts examine their behavior on a regular basis. This is designed to ensure free trade and non-monopolistic behavior.

When BMI started, ASCAP owned the performing rights to virtually everything. At the time ASCAP didn't consider country and blues to be "real," music, and they didn't accept very much jazz either. By welcoming writers of all kinds of music, BMI made tremendous inroads in the pop marketplace. By the rock era of the mid-'50s, BMI was the dominant force. ASCAP fought back by revising its payment programs and openly recruiting folk, country and rock writers. Today there is little difference in musical emphasis between the two organizations, except that ASCAP retains many of the old standards, the pop hits of the 1930s and 1940s.

SESAC was founded in the 1930s. It originally represented primarily Latin American and European copyrights. Several years ago it paid huge advances to Bob Dylan and Neil Diamond, and they switched over to SESAC. SESAC also has a strong presence in the country gospel field, and in general is more visible in the Nashville market.

HOW PERFORMANCE INCOME WORKS

ASCAP and BMI operate similarly to the way political polls function. They do not pretend to accurately record every time a song is played anywhere in the United States. Instead they do logs of radio stations in a sort of proportional way. BMI works directly from radio station logs, and ASCAP does its own independent logging. Each system has its virtues and defects, but the unfortunate fact is that if you are in a niche market, or have a record that is successful only on a regional basis, you will often not show up the surveys of either organization. When your songs are played abroad—on CBC radio in Canada, for example—there are complete logs of everything played on government radio, and you will receive payment for your songs. Many of my friends are niche writers, in such specialized markets as jazz, bluegrass or instrumental music. Those of us who write in these veins often find that our only performing rights income comes from foreign airplay.

If you write hit songs, your material will invariably show up, because you are being played everywhere. With the prevalence of advanced computer programs, watermarks and such reporting companies as Soundscan, it is only a matter of time until everyone is actually compensated according to the specific amount of airplay they receive.

In the meantime major writers don't much care, because they always show up in the logs. Although they will deny it, neither organization does a good job of logging public radio or college radio stations.

SESAC doesn't log, but operates from charts of radio play and record store sales. SESAC does offer advances for songs on records that are in national release. These small advances may in fact exceed the payments that you get from BMI or ASCAP if your writing is in a niche market.

The reader should be aware that a single major hit song can earn hundreds of thousands of dollars, and can continue to provide income over a long period of time if the song continues to receive airplay on radio or television.

WHICH PERFORMING RIGHTS GROUP SHOULD I JOIN?

My suggestion is that you join the organization where you have the best and most receptive contacts. All of the performing rights organizations are capable of opening doors for writers. They can introduce you to music publishers and record companies. The trick is in finding someone at one of these organizations who will take your calls and subsequently comes to believe in your music. Any contact that someone makes for you is a bit risky for them as well. If your work is truly awful, then that publisher is not apt to accept a recommendation from your contact again. Both ASCAP and BMI go to national and regional music meetings and seminars, so it is up to you to hook up with them in any way that you can. In defense of both organizations, I will say that it is much easier to contact them than to deal with the large music publishers or record companies.

BMI and ASCAP both put some of their administrative income into regional music seminars and classes in the major music centers. They also have made sample CDs promoting writers in film and television, and have sponsored songwriters' showcases at various music festivals.

BMI rewards hit writers with additional payments at certain plateaus of airplay. All of the performing rights organizations also license music for jukebox play.

ASCAP has a fund called ASCAP +, which pays money to songwriters whose work is performed live. The songwriter must fill out annual paperwork, indicating when and where the songs were performed, and list any other special credits such as awards or grants received during the year. A panel of music critics analyzes the forms and awards money to writers they deem as deserving more compensation than they are receiving from the organization. Applicants can perform in any musical genre: pop, classical, jazz, rock, etc. The money is paid in addition to any other income derived from ASCAP and is not deducted from other royalty payments.

SESAC has a somewhat similar program, but the applicant must fill out forms for each gig played. BMI has no comparable system at this writing.

For the writer who does not enjoy widespread airplay on major radio stations or who is writing in a niche music style, like bluegrass or modern jazz, it may well be advantageous to join one of the societies that pays for live performances.

SYNCHRONIZATION RIGHTS

There are no specific compulsory fees for these rights. Typically songs in films earn between $15,000 and $25,000, split between the writer and the publisher. It all depends on how strong the song is at the time it is being used, and how it is used in the film. The most significant places for a song are at the beginning and end of a film. These rights cover only the publisher and songwriter. If the original performance is used, the rights for that performance must be negotiated with the record company.

Payment for television synchronization rights also varies. The people who write for the hit TV series, like Mike Post, like to write the theme to the show. The themes will pay performing rights in addition to the one-time synchronization fee. They will continue to do so as the show is rebroadcast on cable TV and in foreign markets.

When a movie is shown, the composer receives no performance royalties while it is shown in movie theaters. The minute the film is shown on television the composer receives performance royalties.

Because so many movie scores today use 15–20 songs, and each song entails a synchronization licensing fee, the income from the placement of songs in movies has become a lucrative aspect of music publishing. When a song is used in a movie in the United States, it does not generate performance income, but when the movie appears on television, that broadcast or broadcasts will generate performance rights to the songwriter and the publisher. In Europe, songwriters and music publishers receive a small percentage of the income from ticket sales.

Commercials that use existing songs can be licensed for specific time periods and for specific areas of the country. They may also be licensed for exclusive uses promoting a product for a given period of time. These rights may pay as much as $500,000 for a national license for a well-known song. The fees will be much less for a regional or local commercial.

BMI and ASCAP also pay for performances in jingles, but there are two caveats to these payments. The first is that the short length of jingles, typically 15-30 seconds, means that the credits for a commercial are a small fraction of what a song generates. It is also common for advertising agencies to pay composers for jingles under the category of works for hire. This means that the agency itself receives income as the composer of the jingle, rather than the money going to the person who composed it.

In smaller cities, songs from records are often illegally used to promote products. People who do this are subject to lawsuits and penalties if they are caught.

PRINT RIGHTS

There are a number of ways that songs may be reprinted by print publishers. They include:

1) The sheet music for hit songs.

2) Folios that include the songs in a particular album.

3) Choral arrangements for high school, junior high school or college choirs.

4) Instrumental versions for pep bands, jazz orchestras or marching bands.

5) Instructional folios for specific instruments, which may reprint contemporary songs or standards.

6) Fake books, which are large collections of songs. used by musicians who play weddings and casuals.

The most active companies in the pop sheet music business are Alfred Music, Mel Bay, Cherry Lane Music, Hal Leonard Corporation and Music Sales. In classical music, Hal Leonard distributes the music of the G. Schirmer Company, and Carl Fischer distributes music published by Theodore Presser. There are other niche companies such as Willis Music, active in the keyboard area; Neil Kjos Music, which specializes in keyboard and school music; Kendor Music, which prints music for college and high school music jazz bands and International Music specializes in classical music.

Although the major record companies and the music publishers who own the publishing rights to songs are in the major music industry cities, the print companies are spread out across the country. Hal Leonard is based in Milwaukee; Alfred Music in Van Nuys, California; Mel Bay in a suburb of St. Louis; Music Sales has offices in New York but the ownership is British; Neil Kjos is in San Diego; Theodore Presser is based in suburban Philadelphia and Carl Fischer in New York.

Print music rights are leased from the publishing company that owns the original copyright. Payment is usually in the 12%-to-20% range, based on the retail selling price. The songwriter should seek to get 50% of this income, but may not always succeed in doing so. Fake book income tends to be quite low, because fake books often contain as many as a thousand songs, with a retail selling price of $35 to $40.

GRAND RIGHTS

Grand rights govern the use of music in theaters. These rights are a percentage of the gross of a play. This percentage is usually anywhere from 4% to 6% of the gross receipts of a play. This income is split between the lyricist, the composer and the author of the book. In most Broadway shows the lyricist and composer are two separate people (unless the author is someone like Stephen Sondheim).

These rights can be enormously lucrative for a small number of writers. As is the case with recordings, most shows are not successful. However, when a show is a hit on Broadway, it can spawn road show companies, international tours, and runs on the West End in London. At a later time there will be dinner theater productions and performances by community theater groups, high schools, and colleges. All of these performances pay royalties. In the case of school and community theater performances, the rates are based on the capacity of a theater.

When pre-existing songs are used in shows, fees are paid for the individual songs. This again depends on the size of the theater and the length of the song.

When songs used in a play are recorded, the other rights prevail. In other words, mechanicals, performance and print rights will all bring in income, as described earlier in this chapter.

ETC.

Songs used in any other way must also be licensed from the publisher. There are no specific fees authorized for music boxes, the reprinting of song lyrics, or greeting cards. All of these rights must be negotiated with the publisher.

In this chapter we have outlined the various sources of income that songs can enjoy. In the next chapter we will turn to the subject of music publishers.

CHAPTER 15 RESOURCES

Two useful books are Tim Whitsett's book *Music Publishing: The Real Road to Music Business Success,* sixth edition, published by Mix Books in 2010, and Jeffrey and Todd Brabec's *Music, Money and Success: The Insider's Guide to the Music Industry,* published by Schirmer Books, sixth edition, 2008.

Music Publishers

WHAT PUBLISHERS DO

Music publishers perform a number of functions on their own behalf, and on behalf of songwriters. These roles include:

1) Paperwork. Publishers copyright songs, keep files of songs, including lead sheets and demos of these songs. They also keep track of the paperwork that is involved when songs are licensed for recordings. They will also generally take the responsibility of paying demo singers and musicians.

2) Publishers act like a bank. They advance money to songwriters who are on staff, based on a weekly or monthly "draw," against royalties. For writers not on staff they may offer advances for individual songs. They also pay for the cost of demos, although often half of these costs are charged against the songwriters' royalties.

3) They maintain offices, staffed with secretaries and with song pluggers, often called professional managers. It is these people who try to get artists to record songs. They also attempt to get songs used in films, license them for commercials, and make deals to lease songs out to print publishers. The larger publishers maintain small offices where songwriters can work on songs, often with collaborators. These offices may include recording equipment and a keyboard instrument.

4) The larger publishers own their own recording studios, where writers can make demos of their songs.

5) Since many writers do not read music and cannot write it down in notation, publishers arrange for trained musicians to write lead sheets, containing the melody lines, chords and words of songs.

6) Some publishers are a valuable source of mentoring and critiques. They may work closely with their writers to polish songs. They may even suggest changes in lyrics or melodies. Depending on the skills of the publisher and the skills and temperament of the writer, these suggestions may be useful or intrusive.

7) Publishers often suggest collaborators whom they regard as possessing skills that are complementary to those of another writer.

8) Publishers may help a new writer network with other writers, artists, producers and record company personnel in the hopes of helping the writers to develop and expand the scope of their careers.

9) Publishers will be vigilant about the payment of royalties from record companies and any other income sources. Most publishers utilize the Harry Fox office to license music and to collect royalties.

That office charges publishers a fee that is set each year. It is generally in the vicinity of 3% to 5%, which is charged against both the writer and the publisher. The Fox Agency also advises publishers about synchronization rights, and can execute those licenses as well.

10) Publishers generally subscribe to "tip sheets." These little newsletters list artists and producers who are looking for songs for specific recording projects. Tip sheets are extremely expensive; few songwriters would want to spent the $150 to $200 a year it costs to get one of them.

11) Professional managers have their own network of industry contacts. Through constant interaction with producers, artist and repertoire personnel at record companies, personal managers and even artists, they keep close track of who is doing what. They also follow through to see which of the songs that artists are considering actually get recorded, and whether they end up on albums or become singles.

12) Music publishers may assist record companies in promoting a group that writes all of its own songs. In other words, let's say Warner Chappell owns the publishing of a group that records for Sony. In addition to the efforts of the normal Sony promotion staff, Warner Chappell may hire some independent promotion people to assist in the project, at no expense to Sony. The reason for doing this is that the publisher will enjoy considerable income if the group is successful.

13) Some music publishers may assist artists who also write songs in obtaining recording contracts. In a case where the publishing company owns a recording studio, it may even hire a producer and make finished master recordings, which they then attempt to sell to a record company.

14) Music publishers also cultivate relationships with music supervisors, the people who place songs in films or on television shows. The songwriter is not apt to have these contacts on her own.

DO YOU NEED A PUBLISHER?

This is a difficult question to answer. Look at the list of publisher functions above, and decide for yourself whether you are qualified or interested in fulfilling all or any of these functions. Highly successful writers may hire their own office staff to do this work. Are you in a position to pay someone, and to rent office space to do all of this? Or are you willing to do it all yourself?

Keep in mind that there are only so many hours in a day. If you are going to pursue all of these publisher functions, will you have time to actually write songs? For songwriters in the early stages of their careers, it is generally foolish to attempt to publish their own songs. On the other hand, if you have good industry contacts with artists and producers and enjoy pitching your own songs, publishing can prove to be a lucrative pursuit.

STAFF WRITING DEALS

When a writer is a staff writer, he or she gets paid a weekly or monthly draw, an advance against royalties. These advances are generally in the range of $300 to $500 a week. In return for this advance, all of the writer's work is published by the publishing company. Most of these deals are like record contracts in the sense that the publisher has options to renew the contract for two to four additional years. If the publisher is not successful in obtaining recordings of the writer's music, then the deal will probably end at the end of the first year. Sometimes these deals require the writer to deliver a set number of "commercially acceptable" songs each year. If these are co-written songs, they only count as a percentage of a required song. In other words, if you have a single co-writer, the song is equivalent to half of a song required to be delivered.

SONGPLUGGERS

There are several alternatives to having a publisher for someone who wants to retain her own publishing but doesn't want to do all the legwork it takes to get a song recorded. In Nashville it is quite common to use songpluggers, who represent individual songs or even an entire catalog of songs. According to the book *Songplugger: The Cuts and the Bruises*, referenced at the end of the chapter, songpluggers are paid in different ways. Some work without a fee, taking a percentage of any song they get recorded. It is more common to pay a monthly retainer to a songplugger, which ranges from $300 to $700 a month. In addition to this fee the plugger will want to receive a percentage bonus on each song that gets recorded, and additional bonuses if the song is released as a single, makes the charts, etc.

Although there are unscrupulous songpluggers who will sign a song and not do much of anything to place it, many of them have had considerable success in placing songs. It is best to check with other songwriters or the performing rights organizations to see if the songplugger has a legitimate track record. Some writers who are signed to publishers use songpluggers as an additional resource to get songs recorded. This is because a publisher may have a number of writers under contract, in addition to a back catalog that may contain hundreds or even thousands of songs. Songpluggers usually report their activities to the writer on a regular basis.

In Los Angeles there are songwriters' managers. They work for a percentage of the songwriters' revenue.

IS THERE A DOWNSIDE TO HAVING A PUBLISHER?

There are several negatives in having a music publisher.

First of all, you are going to give up HALF of your income from your songs. This can amount to a considerable amount of money. Remember, we are talking about half of your entire songwriting income—record royalties, performance rights, synchronization rights, etc.

A more subtle but still important problem is that some artists, producers and record companies will refuse to record songs that they don't own themselves. In other words, they will want to publish your songs. If your songs are already published by someone else, you have no flexibility in such negotiations.

REVERSION CLAUSES

If you do sign a deal with a publisher, you should try to get a reversion clause in the contract. A reversion clause states that the songs return to the writer after a specified period of time if the publisher is unable to get the song or songs recorded. The publisher will want to extend this period as long as possible, while the writer will want to make it as short a time as possible. The publisher will maintain, with some accuracy, that it takes time to build the reputation of a writer, and that they have invested money in the writer. It is up to you to determine what constitutes a reasonable period of time. Something like a year sounds right to me, although it is true that some songs have been around for seven or eight years before anyone has recorded them.

THE BOTTOM LINE

You need to weigh the advantages and disadvantages of having a publisher. It is obvious that early in your career it is advantageous to have a helping hand. We will soon explore some other possibilities that will enable you to retain a portion of your publishing rights, but let's proceed to discussing how you can find a music publisher in the first place.

FINDING A PUBLISHER

There are a number of ways to find a music publisher. In order to get one you will need some demos of your songs. It is wise to have a tape or CDR that includes no more than three songs. Be sure that the song that you think is your strongest one is the first one on the tape. If the publisher dislikes your first song, they may never listen to the second or third song.

Let's assume that you have a reasonable demo with your three best songs, and you also have lyric sheets that you can submit to the publisher, not written in longhand but printed out from some sort of word processing program. Below are some ways of finding a publisher.

1) An annual publication called *Songwriter's Market* is a valuable resource for finding a music publisher. It gives the name and address of the company, what sort of songs they publish and examples of songs that they have published that have been recorded. It is available in hard copy or on a CD-ROM.

If you use *Songwriter's Market,* you need to exercise a bit of common sense. Anyone can establish a music publishing company by registering with a Secretary of State's office in a particular state and paying a small fee. If you see a company that is, for example, based in Lewiston, Idaho, that claims to publish rap music, you ought to be skeptical of their influence and contacts.

You also will notice that some large companies listed in *Songwriter's Market* state that they will not accept unsolicited material. All publishers listed accept unsolicited submissions. Some large publishers do not want to accept such submissions, for two reasons: One, they are concerned about the possibility of frivolous lawsuits if your song happens to have a lyric or theme similar to that of another song

that they may publish down the line. Two, they simply do not want to spend their time handling dozens, hundreds or thousands of songs from sources that they know nothing about. Quite a few publishers prefer to go on recommendations from musicians, artists, record company staff or managers.

Songwriter's Market investigates any complaints from writers about rip-offs, and one of the editors has told me that if they receive two complaints they generally remove the publisher from the next edition of the book.

2) We have already mentioned that ASCAP, BMI and SESAC all can provide an entrée to music publishers. The addresses for these organizations are in the appendix of this book. You need to be aware of the fact that they will not refer all writers, but only the ones they consider to be talented and ready for relatively immediate exposure.

3) Many cities have open-mike situations. In these free-form club situations you can often meet other writers and musicians who may have contacts with music publishers beyond your own network of affiliations. Naturally, places like the Bluebird Cafe in Nashville will be more fruitful for such contacts than an open-mike night in Moose Jaw, Saskatchewan. Often open-mike nights are a better place to find future collaborators than publishers.

4) Regional music seminars, such as South by Southwest in Austin, North by Northwest in Portland, Oregon, or similar events in Philadelphia, New Orleans, Vancouver and other cities, often are attended by publishers and by representatives from performing rights organizations. This is your chance to meet these people and make initial contacts that can lead to fruitful relationships. Some of these seminars even have song critique sessions, where music publishers evaluate songs.

5) Regional music organizations are another avenue for making contacts with both music publishers and collaborators. NSAI, the Nashville Songwriters Association International, holds seminars, has rooms for writers, and is active in educating songwriters about the music business. It also has regional branches that offer similar, if lower-level, services.

You can find a list of major songwriting organizations in the appendix of this book. To find local songwriting organizations, I recommend that you consult *Songwriter's Market*, the Musician's Atlas, local music publications or performing rights organizations. Local or regional songwriter's organizations can provide a support base for your work. You should be able to find other writers who can help you to develop your skills. You can also find collaborators at their meetings. Many of these groups also sponsor meetings where publishers come in and offer critiques and general information about the business of songwriting.

6) Local bands in your area who have recording and/or publishing deals may be a source of publishing contacts, and they also may provide you with the opportunity to record your songs. Of course, many of these groups record only their own material, but even in such cases there may be co-writing opportunities available to you.

It is important for the songwriter to understand that even if he or she has a music publisher, the writer should utilize their own contacts to help get songs recorded. Many songwriters have friendships with record producers and artists, and this informal interaction can be very effective in getting songs recorded or placed in films or television.

SONG SHARKS

At this point I need to warn you about a special species of publisher known as the song shark. Anytime you copyright songs, you are apt to get letters from mysterious sources informing you that for a fee they will put your song on a record that will go to radio stations and recording artists. Songwriters should *never* agree to pay fees to get their songs out in the world. It is the other way around: You should receive royalties for your songs. No legitimate music publisher will make such demands.

These folks are quite slippery, and they will actually fulfill their promises, but in a way that is useless to you. They will place your song on a CD with the work of other unknown writers, and they will indeed send them to radio stations and record companies. The CDs and your song will end up in company wastebaskets, because these useless submissions are sent out on a regular basis. They will not fool professionals in the business.

My favorite story of how ruthless these people are is related by a writer, publisher and producer named Shad O'Shea in a book that he wrote called *For the Record*. On being informed that he was a writer of "great talent," O'Shea submitted a song whose entire lyric was "Ooh baby, ooh." He received a return letter complimenting him on his wonderful song, and stating that for a fee the company would place it on a recording.

Similarly I read a story in the Astoria, Oregon, newspaper *The Daily Astorian* about a woman who fell for this routine. The company kept telling her how great she was, and explaining that her song was so good that they wanted to add string parts and background vocals. All of this cost several thousand dollars. Unfortunately, she fell for this line, and emptied out a considerable portion of her life savings in the hopes of having a hit country song. Not only was the song never released on a recording, but when the poor writer tried to follow up with phone calls she found out that the telephone was disconnected and the company had disappeared.

This story is more extreme than most, because most of the song sharks stay within the letter of the law. They simply are of no use to you, and I strongly suggest that you avoid them.

TAXI advertises that some of its writers from obscure corners of the country have achieved placements through the organization, but undoubtedly, many others have not enjoyed comparable success. TAXI charges a fee of $300 for its services, plus a small fee for each song submitted. Submitted songs receive written critiques, which may be useful to the writer. TAXI certainly utilizes contacts an unknown writer is probably not privy to. It is up to the writer to decide whether to find a publisher, develop contacts on his own or use TAXI.

There are a number of legitimate services, such as TAXI, that employ professionals to listen to your songs, critique them, and provide industry contacts. Some competent professional songwriters offer similar services. Personally I am uncomfortable with the notion that someone should have to pay to have songs critiqued. I certainly recommend that you be skeptical of anyone who charges you money for such services.

COPYRIGHTING YOUR SONGS

Anytime I have taught a class or a seminar on the music business, I am invariably asked how to copyright songs, and whether it is wise to do so. To copyright an individual song costs $35 if you file electronically, and $65 if you file with hard copy. You get one of two forms from the Library of Congress, form PA or SR. If you use form PA, you must write out the words and melody line of the song. Form SR actually copyrights the sound recording, but also serves as protection for the song. When you use SR you send a copy of a cassette with your song on it along with the form. (See the appendix for the correct address.)

There is another way to copyright songs that is cheaper. You can use form SR and record up to ten songs on a cassette. Be sure that the tape has you saying the title before each song. You need to title the song as a collection, for example "Spring Songs by Dan Fox." The fee for the entire tape is $35, quite a bit less than the per-song fee.

If one of the songs on your tape gets recorded, it is a good idea to copyright that song separately. It will cost you another $35, but if your song is being recorded it's a good investment.

Now let's look at the second question. Should you copyright your song? You need to examine your paranoia quotient, and also the question of whom you are sending your songs to. I tend to be most paranoid about sending songs to people or companies I have never heard of. I take the position, wisely or unwisely, that companies like Warner Chappell have better things to do than to rip off my songs. If you worry about this sort of thing, by all means copyright *all* of your songs.

ARE THERE OTHER FORMS OF COPYRIGHT?

In a word, no. Do not send yourself copies of your songs in sealed envelopes. This will not hold up in court, because it is possible that you could have inserted material at a later date by steaming open the envelope. I have read that in England this form of copyright is good in court. I don't know whether that is true, but don't try it in the USA.

CAN I USE A TINY BIT OF ANOTHER SONG?

Somewhere in the underground grapevine of songwriters there circulates an idea that you can use up to four bars of somebody else's songs without legal repercussions. Don't. It isn't true. The way the copyright law is written, it is an infringement if there is substantial similarity. If you use a recognizable four-bar figure, even something as simple as the melody to the words *Hey Jude,* you will be sued. You will in all likelihood lose.

SAMPLING

If you sample other people's songs it is possible to work out agreements with the original publishers and/or record companies in which you pay for the samples. If you use extensive samples you will end up not owning any of the song at all.

INFRINGEMENTS AND LAWSUITS

There are two things that govern successful copyright actions: substantial similarity between one song and another, and access. If you think that an artist has ripped off your song, you must prove not only that the words or music are similar, but also that a reasonable person would accept that the artist had access to your song.

George Harrison of the Beatles lost the suit on his song "My Sweet Lord" because it was determined that when he was a teenager he listened to BBC Radio, and they were playing a song with a similar melody called "He's So Fine."

In exceptional circumstances a court can waive the access provisions. This might happen, for example, if someone came up with a song exactly like a complex, well-known work, like the melody of a current symphonic work. Under most conditions, both similarity and access must be proved by the complainant.

COPUBLISHING

Earlier in the chapter I mentioned that there are alternatives to giving up all of your publishing rights. The most common alternative is called copublishing. In copublishing you retain your rights as a songwriter (50% of the pie) and you also receive some percentage, usually 50% of the publishing rights. This means that you now own 75% of the song, instead of the 50% that the writer with a publishing agreement usually has.

Generally copublishing is available to writers with a proven track record of success. The writer may also have extensive contacts in the artist and production community. Under such circumstances the publisher understands that the writer himself will be able to do many of the song-plugging tasks that the publisher normally expects to undertake.

Copublishing can also be achieved when a new group that writes its own music appears that has developed the fabled big-time industry "buzz." In other words, several record companies are competing for the services of the group, which is generally believed to be a hot commodity. A shrewd and well-connected manager can attempt to use the group's music publishing as a bargaining chip in the record deal. The manager can either hold out to keep half of the publishing, or can keep all of it, and sell off half of it to a publishing company for an advance. This might be a useful tack if the group needs to buy a new van, recording equipment or expensive microphones. A group in Colorado called the Subdudes used this ploy and was able to sell half of its publishing when several different record companies were in a bidding war to sign them.

Because record companies are struggling to find more

income streams as album sales decline, labels will almost certainly increase pressure on new acts to sign all or half of their publishing rights to the record company.

ADMINISTERING THE COPYRIGHT

In copublishing deals the consideration of who administers the copyright can be important. The person who administers the copyright gets to make decisions on such questions as whether to use songs in commercials. Some writers strongly object to such uses, or at least want input into making the decisions.

As long as the relationship between the copublishers is good, this is not usually a problem. But imagine a situation with a copublishing deal where the two companies no longer are in business together, and possibly dislike one another. Say that someone whose songs have seriously religious content, like Amy Grant, makes a copublishing deal with Greed and Grime Music. When the relationship dissolves, they each go their own way. Three years later the director of a porno film wants to use a song that Amy Grant wrote in his movie. Since there is no longer a relationship between the publisher and Amy or her management group, they license this use. This would be extremely damaging to the career of a Christian artist, and undoubtedly would cause her considerable pain. Yet it is perfectly legal if Greed and Grime are the administrators of the copyright.

It is possible in administration deals for the publishers to have mutual power, but this can be clumsy and awkward if there is a complex negotiation going on for, say, a particular movie use.

ADMINISTRATION DEALS

When an artist-writer is a superstar, he may own all of his own publishing. Since very few songwriters want to spend their time doing office work, they will then subcontract the paperwork to a law firm or an existing publishing company. They will pay a small percentage of the gross income for these services, usually 5% to 10% of the gross. The writer will also pay any expenses incurred in administration. Under these circumstances the writer now enjoys 80% to 90% of the total income. Sometimes such deals are crafted so that if the administrator actually solicits new recordings of the writer's songs, they get some additional percentage of royalties. This percentage will be for that recording alone, not for any other future recordings of the song.

WHAT'S THE BEST DEAL?

Of course it's advantageous to keep as much of your publishing as possible. Still, 100% of nothing, as the saying goes, is nothing. If you find publishers who are working hard to promote your career, who are helping you to make contacts, finding you collaborators, and getting your songs into movies or television products, maybe you should consider the possibility that they really are earning their money.

In the next chapter we'll consider another possibility: doing it all yourself.

CHAPTER 16 RESOURCES

The book on songpluggers referred to in this capter is Penny Dionne's and Troy McConnell's book, *Songplugger: The Cuts and the Bruises*.

Tim Whitsett's *The Real Road to Music Business Success*, sixth edition, 2010, is a good resource for most of your questions about music publishing. So is the the latest edition of *Music, Money and Success*, sixth edition, 2008, by Jeffrey Brabec and Todd Brabec.

Operating Your Own Music Publishing Company

This chapter is intended for those who choose to operate their own music publishing company. You may have elected to go in this direction because you prefer to enjoy all of the income, or possibly you would like to find a music publisher but no one is receptive to your work. Another possibility is that you have watched what your previous publisher did to promote your music, and you feel that you can do a better job of promoting your songs than he did.

WHERE TO START

If you live outside the major music markets and don't have the financial wherewithal to visit them on a regular basis, there are still some fruitful strategies that you can pursue. Look for a local artist or band that is interested in listening to material from outside writers. You may hire these folks to do your demos, and even pay them to do so. Many such artists are making their own CDs these days. Because you know them, they are probably fairly accessible to you. In a regional music market, chances are that writers aren't beating their doors down offering them new songs.

Once your song is recorded, assuming that the recording is reasonably good, you have a little more of a track record with which you can approach publishers. If you still want to own all of the rights to the songs, you can start sending this CD out to artists, producers and managers. In other words, you are acting like a professional manager of a publishing company.

KEEPING RECORDS

It is a good idea to develop some sort of data base that enables you to keep track of whom you are pitching songs to. It might look like this:

Name of Song

_____

Date written

_____

Copyrighted?

_____

Cowriter, if any

_____

Sent out to

_____

Phone query on status

_____

Placed on hold by

_____

Date of hold

_____

Call regarding status & response

_____

Recorded by

_____

Name of label, date of release

_____

Cover records

_____

If you do additional pitches of the song, you may want to use another page.

HOW TO PITCH SONGS TO AN ARTIST OR PRODUCER

How do you find a particular artist or producer? Buy their most recent album, and check for the producer's name. If the producer is well-known, he probably has an office and a production company. To reach the artist, find out who is managing them. The *Billboard Talent & Touring Directory* is an annual publication that should have this information. If necessary, you can contact the artist's record company and ask to get their manager's address.

The manager, producer or artist will probably ask you if your songs are already published. When you say they aren't, they will very likely pressure you to give them the publishing rights. You can say yes or no, or you can ask for a copublishing deal. It is difficult to tell whether your unwillingness to give them publishing on the song will

keep them from recording it. It's a bluffing game of sorts. Other ways of finding artists are through tour managers, musicians in the band, and even some of the audio personnel. The problem with this is that the further you get from someone with direct contact and influence over an artist, the more likely it is that your tape will disappear before the artist ever hears it. Other sources who *may* have some connection to an artist are disc jockeys, promoters, club owners and opening acts for the artist you are trying to reach.

It is always possible to pitch songs through the mail, but it is less effective. You are not going to be able to judge whether anyone close to the artist actually listened to your demo.

PROFESSIONALISM

If you are forming your own music publishing company, it is important that you operate in as professional a way as you possibly can. Everything from your stationery and company logo (if you have one) to the way you package your tapes and the quality of your lyric sheets will stamp you as a professional or a wannabe. When you work for yourself you need to make all of the decisions, whether they concern your music or the color of your business cards.

COMPANY NAMES

You will need to clear your company name with one of the performing rights organizations. In my most recent publishing venture my first company name didn't clear. I was surprised that the second name, Long Bridge Music, did clear. Try to come up with an original name that isn't too close to the name of an existing publishing company. It is also helpful if the name is either humorous or somehow relates to the type of music you write. River Run Music might be a reasonable name for a new age publisher, but it wouldn't be a good choice for a rap company. Hardball Music might be a better option for a rap company.

THE NATURE OF HOLDS

When a publisher puts a song on hold, it means that an artist is interested in recording the song. As a courtesy to that artist, the publisher agrees not to show the song around until the artist has recorded it. The publisher, by the way, can control the first recording of a song. All subsequent recordings can be legally made by anyone, provided that they pay royalties for the songs.

The problem with holds is that an artist may have a dozen songs on hold, and have only two open spots in their next CD. You walk around excited about the forthcoming recording, but in fact it isn't likely that it will happen.

Another common problem is that the artist may delay his plans to record an album, but still wants to keep a song on hold. This delay may last for months, and meanwhile the songwriter and publisher have given up the chance for other artists to record the song. Sometimes the song is recorded and even mixed but the artist has recorded too many songs for a single album, and your song may fall by the wayside. It is also possible that the artist intends to record a song, and may even do so, but the record company drops the artist and does not issue the recording.

I once had an experience with a producer putting a hold on a song. He went into the studio with a new artist who totally froze in the studio, and was essentially unable to sing. The record company dropped the artist, the producer forgot about my song, and I was frustrated. It's all part of the game.

If an artist or producer puts several of your songs on

hold, doesn't call you, and then doesn't record them, you can always adopt the tactic of not offering them any more songs. Then you can hope that they don't produce any major artists for whom you happen to have the perfect song!

According to the *Songplugger* book cited in the last chapter of this book, some publishers are beginning to fight back by telling an artist or producer that a hold is only good for a certain period of time, for example, two weeks. If the publisher hasn't heard from the artist, their producer or manager by then, they contact the artist or producer with a reminder that the hold is going to expire unless they make a definite commitment to record the song.

MATCHING SONGS WITH ARTISTS

The only way that you can learn to match songs with artists is by following the evolution of an artist's career and trying to move in the direction that you think that he or she is moving in. If the artist changes producers from one album to the next, or in midstream, all of your careful planning may become irrelevant. All you can do is listen carefully, and try to write as appropriately as you can for that artist.

Some artists have specific lyrics or styles of lyrics that they favor. Celine Dion, for example, often records songs with the word "love" in the title. So your task here is to come up with a romantic power ballad that utilizes her sense of drama and extensive vocal range. It isn't rocket science, but it's easier to describe than to do.

ATTORNEYS

Music business attorneys constitute a small percentage of the legal profession. They seem to know everyone at the record companies and music publishers. If you are doing business with a music industry attorney, find out whether they have some contacts that you can exploit. Do these people really know anything about music? For the most part the answer is no. What they can do is to put you in touch with decision makers.

DEMOS

Since you are your own publisher, you are also the person who is in charge of making demos of your songs. Do you want a male or a female singer to demo you song? It may be that you will need both sorts of demos. Chances are that the two singers will sing the song in different keys. So not only will you have to cut two different vocal tracks, but you may very well have to cut two separate instrumental versions of the song.

You will need to pay the musicians, and you are better off using professionals who are sympathetic to the style of music that you write in than to ask your friends to contribute their services for free. Your "friends" may end up costing you a fortune in studio time, often far more than what you would have paid a professional.

VOCAL AND INSTRUMENTAL PERFORMANCES

Even if you cut some really brilliant instrumental tracks, it is the lead vocal that will sell or destroy your song. You need to get used to working with singers and getting the best possible performance out of them. Most musicians and vocalists have a sense of pride, and will do their best. However, if you don't instruct them carefully about what you want, you will get their interpretation of the song rather than the one you had in mind.

Developing a rapport with musicians and singers is a process that takes time and a certain amount of diplomacy. If you make performers angry, they will generally become defensive and resort to devices that will get the job done, but almost certainly will not enhance your song.

When you ask musicians to bring certain instruments to a session, it is important that you know exactly what you want. Do you want a twelve-string guitar, a classical guitar, an acoustic-electric? You need to do your homework or you will suffer the consequences.

DEMO SERVICES

There are a number of demo services scattered throughout the United States. Often these are musicians who have a pro tools set-up or who own one or two ADAT machines and play several instruments, including a synthesizer. Personally, I would *never* send a song to be demoed by someone whom I don't know who is working in another city. Often these sorts of demos are reasonably professional; they simply sound like many other songs. If you can find a demo service where you live, and if you can be there to give input at the sessions, then it may prove worthwhile for you.

The good news is that this expenditure of time and money will enable you to develop production skills that may lead you into a whole other career.

DEMO PAYMENTS

If you record with union musicians, which will often be the case in Nashville or Los Angeles, there is a scale for demos. It is currently $35 an hour in Los Angeles, with the session leader getting 50% more, or $52.50 an hour. There is a 10% payment to the pension fund, a $5 payment for health and welfare, and fees for playing more than one instrument and multiple parts. Singers are usually paid about $50 a tune. The union scale for demos varies in different cities, and is set locally.

In smaller markets many musicians may not belong to the union, so you must negotiate payments with them. In my opinion, it is a mistake to underpay musicians, and you often will get exactly what you pay for.

DO YOU STILL WANT TO DO THIS?

Owning your own music publishing operation gives you absolute creative and business control over your songs. It also requires that you spend a good deal of time hustling, and offers you no guaranteed income. It is up to you to make the decision. Whatever you do, keep an open mind, and be willing to change your mind if it is in your own best interests to do so.

CHAPTER 17 RESOURCES

Fred Koller's book *How To Pitch & Promote Your Songs,* published by Allworth Press in 1996, details many of the realities of running your own music publishing company.

Songwriting Tips

COMBINING THE WORDS AND THE MUSIC

We've already had some discussions about whether the words, the music, the rhythms or the ideas come first. You should recall that we answered that question by saying "any of the above." When a song is in the final revision process, there are some things to look at. Some of them include:

1) Do any of the words stick out uncomfortably because they're hard to sing?

2) Do the lyrics and the melody fit well together?

3) Does the song deliver what it promised? The function of the first verse is to set the mood for the song. Did the succeeding verses follow through on that beginning?

4) Is the chorus the part of the song that is easiest to remember? Does it focus the subject of the song?

5) Do the verses and the chorus go together, or do they seem like two different songs that were glued together?

6) Is there anything you need to add or subtract in your final version? Is there a need for a bridge? Is the bridge accomplishing something besides representing a diversion?

7) Does the song have universal, or at least general,

meaning? Some songs are so personal and autobiographical that they are meaningless to others.

8) Is the voice of the singer-narrator consistent? In most instances if you start by using the second person "you," you want to stay with that. If the song has dialogue between different characters, one of whom is "I," this may not be the case.

9) If you are trying to write "commercial" songs, are there hooks in the song that will bring the listener into the story or the tune?

10) What artist do you think would be appropriate to sing this song?

11) What sort of audience do you think will find the song entertaining or insightful?

12) How do you plan to market the song?

COMBINING CAREERS AS A WRITER AND AN ARTIST

Many songwriters end up being artists. This may be by design or by accident. Often a songwriter can put a particular level of feeling in a song that no one else seems to be able to match. Many songwriters, such as John Denver or Karla Bonoff, were signed as artists on the strength of their songwriting abilities. Denver's first big hit was the Peter, Paul & Mary recording of "Leaving On A Jet Plane," while Bonoff wrote several hits for Linda Ronstadt. Other writers became artists through their success as record producers, as did Babyface.

It is probably worth mentioning that some writers are really better off not becoming recording artists, and many of them understand that. Performing involves developing and promoting an image, as well as musical factors. Some great writers are simply unsuited to be performers, or prefer not to perform. Nevertheless, some writers who are better off not performing still feel a compulsion to do it. It's so much easier to get cuts on your own recordings and not have to hustle other artists or producers to record your songs.

Another career option is to put the skills to work that you learned in making demos and produce records for yourself and/or other people. In today's music world, many people have developed careers as writers, artists and producers. They move comfortably from one role to another, depending on the demand for their services and their own desire to try on different hats. Kanye West, Jimmy Jam and Terry Lewis, and T-Bone Burnett are among many talented musicians who have elected not to limit their musical focus to a single area.

THE ECONOMIC IMPERATIVE

You have probably already figured out why a songwriter who is a mediocre (or worse) singer becomes a recording artist. By becoming an artist, a writer solves several immediate problems.

1) There is now a finished recording of the writer's songs, which can serve as an ultimate demo. Ultimate in the sense that no publisher (or writer) in their right mind would spend, say, $15,000 on a demo. Since most records have approximately ten songs and the cost of making a major album is about $250,000 or more these days, I have designated $25,000 as the cost of producing each song.

2) The publisher saves a bundle. The publisher doesn't have to front demo costs, and yet has an excellent finished product to promote.

3) One cannot predict the future. How many people would have predicted tremendous success for Bob Dylan as a singer rather than as a writer? Although his first hits were recorded by Peter, Paul & Mary, he subsequently had plenty of hit singles and albums of his own. Sometimes the public really enjoys a singer of "modest" vocal ability who has a unique way of getting the emotional nuances across in his or her songs.

4) Sometimes a writer underestimates his vocal talents, and by singing on a regular basis grows to become a much better singer than he ever imagined he would be.

ANOTHER STRATEGY

Another strategy for the vocally impaired songwriter who is a decent musician is to join a band as a player rather than a singer. In this way the songwriter can become involved in the arranging and recording of his songs, and has a ready outlet for his work. Unfortunately, it is rarely this simple. It is not unusual for the people in a band to invariably appoint themselves as the lead singer for any songs that they have written. Never mind that three other members of the band do it better! It's a plain and simple ego trip, and it isn't a good idea. Bands should treat each song as though it were an outside song, coming from a writer who is not a band member. The person who should sing the lead is the person who is the best singer. In practice this may or may not be the writer of the song.

OTHER ADVANTAGES OF BAND MEMBERSHIP

Being in a band offers other advantages beyond cowriting

opportunities. Rehearsals with bassists, guitar players, piano players and drummers allows you the opportunity to develop arrangements of your songs over a period of time. Many of these arrangements can then be tried out in front of a live audience.

When you're not in a band the typical demo session is thrown together with very little notice. Although the musicians and singers may be professionals, their investment in the performance, not to mention the expense of studio time and session fees, virtually guarantees that you will end up with a reasonable, but not exciting final product. There also is generally little time and money available to mix the song down to its optimum final form.

COWRITING AS AN ECONOMIC IMPERATIVE

In or out of a band, cowriting is one way to make sure that you get songs on records. If you are in a band, it is a common practice to cowrite with the lead singer, who then becomes more interested and involved in recording your songs. Think of Mick Jagger and Keith Richards—the singer and guitarist are the cowriters of virtually all of the songs recorded by the Rolling Stones.

Another advantage of collaboration is that each writer can utilize their contacts with artists, record producers and music supervisors for film and television to market a song. Since collaborators often have different music publishers, this may mean that now four people are out there promoting the song instead of two.

POINTS OF VIEW AND THE QUESTION OF AUTOBIOGRAPHY

In Bill Flanagan's book *Written in My Soul,* the late blues composer Willie Dixon stated that when writing he tried to project how someone else feels. Rather than writing about himself, he tried to think about how he would feel if the particular situation described had happened to him.

Autobiographical songs are a touchy subject. Many writers end up feeling that they have revealed too much about themselves. On the other hand, writers like Jewel or Fiona Apple seem to delight in describing their personal dilemmas. My hunch is that young writers have a tendency to think that anything that has happened to them will fascinate an audience. Older writers are more protective of their privacy.

There are also writers who glorify in crucifying the former objects of their interpersonal relationships. Joni Mitchell points out in Flanagan's book that when she started writing in the second person, substituting "you" for "I," many of her fans were annoyed. They felt as though she had become judgmental and accusatory rather than revealing her own emotions.

CREATIVITY AND WRITING STYLE

It is very difficult to set up rules and conditions for creativity. It is also probably useless. Only you can work out a methodology of working that is useful for you. Here are some of the questions that you may want to examine:

1) Are you the sort of writer who writes a little bit at a time, or does that sort of technique make you lose the impetus and enthusiasm for completing a project?

2) What are the physical conditions that are conducive for you to write? Do you need to travel, to set up a room that is your major writing place, or do you need an office space separate from your home?

3) Do you write best on impulse, or are you a "deadline writer"? The deadline writer, like the typical

college student, can only work when facing a recording deadline. This sort of person stays up all night and does the work, and may very well do it well. Other creative people may function on a more regular basis, and cannot turn out work in an assembly-line manner.

4) Are you lazy? Is it hard to motivate yourself to work? If this is a recurrent problem, you may turn to collaboration, and you may want to choose a sort of no-nonsense collaborator who is a workaholic.

5) Do you do a good job of exploiting your own talents? If you are a really good guitarist, for example, are you taking advantage of that skill in integrating instrumental lines into your songs, and are you playing on the demos?

ELIMINATING BARRIERS

Try to eliminate recurrent annoyances that interfere with your ability to work. In Flanagan's interview with Van Morrison, Morrison points out that when he has to deal with the business of music, it impedes his creativity. If this is true for you, try to separate the business side of your life from the creative aspects. You can do this by working through a music publisher, or by setting aside times when you perform each of these functions, taking care to separate them. In other words, don't have a stress-filled meeting with a record producer and try to write songs on the same day. On the other hand, some creative people thrive on pressure, and a negative experience simply provides more fodder for their creativity. Only you can decide what is the best way for you to work.

Avoid constantly ringing cell phones, don't answer faxes and don't consult e-mail when you are working. Try to keep your family life separate from your work. This is one of the primary advantages of a separate work space.

Some writers like to baby themselves with chocolate treats, special meals or massages after they feel they've done a good day's work. I personally feel that this is somewhat juvenile, but if it is a good way for you to work, by all means do it.

MOOD

Mood is another one of those indefinable things that can make a song work or destroy it. Dylan told Flanagan that when he puts something on paper and then puts it away, he often finds that he can't finish it. This is because whatever his emotional and mental process was at the time, he can't recapture it at another time. The notebook writer would most likely have an opposite opinion. Such a writer would maintain that getting some distance from a song and taking it apart makes it that much better. It is possible that this distance may result in a new perspective, or even in adding new elements to a song.

CODED MESSAGES AND MULTI-LEVEL WRITING

Using a coded message is a technique that was used in writing black spirituals in the nineteenth century. The master heard the slaves singing and dancing, and didn't have a clue that they were talking about running away, because a particular song referred to a route on the Underground Railway that carried slaves to freedom. Similarly when Curtis Mayfield wrote the song "Keep On Pushing," many people probably didn't grasp his metaphor about tearing down the walls of racial discrimination.

Rap writers or others who write songs intended for young people achieve a similar result in a less subtle way by utilizing or inventing new slang terms that older people don't understand. Thus, references to drugs or illegal behavior may go right over the heads of radio programmers and the general public.

There is, however, a more literary aspect of writing, one that takes place on more than one level. This is a more complex way of approaching songwriting, where you talk about something that makes perfect sense to the uneducated listener but operates on another level for the person that looks below the surface of the song. In Lou Reed's interview with Flanagan, Reed describes his objective as having a plot below the surface of his lyrics, as well as the obvious one. For him, using more than one level of writing and keeping a song fun are the main goals in his songwriting.

The sort of writer who has an interest in subplots, ambiguity or complexity is generally the kind who has a strong interest in literature and other art forms and brings this into his writing. The question then becomes whether it is necessary for the listener to share this knowledge in order to understand the writer's songs. When this sort of thing is done artfully, the subplots, metaphors or similes may sail way over the head of the average listener, yet that person may love what is readily understandable in the song. So when Dylan talks about the answer blowin' in the wind, you can let that symbolism fly right by you, you can interpret the wind as the changes taking place in the nation in the 1960s, or you can simply take it as a literary, naturalistic reference that is non-specific. Does this make the song better? I suppose that this is a matter of opinion, but I would maintain that it certainly makes the song more interesting.

If the use of metaphors, obscure cultural references, or similar devices is done thoughtlessly, it only tends to confuse the listener. It may also make the consumer feel that the writer is pretentious or arrogant. It comes down to the question of whom you are writing for, and whether you are concerned with the question of commercial success.

THE CONFUSION OF ARTISTRY AND COMMERCIALITY

There are writers who never get anything recorded who are convinced that it is because their work is too deep, or goes beyond the level of mediocrity that so many songs exude. There are also writers and publishers who constantly cite hit songs to writers as though they represent some sort of Holy Grail that young writers should strive for. In trying to look at these problems objectively, I have a few observations. First of all, I maintain that there is little relationship between what is commercially successful and what is artistically valid. What I mean is that some songs that are big hits, like, for example "Walkin' In Memphis" by Mark Cohn, are also artistically satisfying. I am not, however, convinced that it is necessarily the artistic qualities of songs that result in making them commercially successful. There are too many elements in what goes before the public— questions like whether a song is adequately promoted by the record company, whether a recording's production is so compelling that we find ourselves enjoying the multiple plays that radio gives a song, or whether an artist's performance is so emotionally satisfying that we find ourselves humming and enjoying a thoroughly mediocre song. There is also little question in my mind that artists who attain a certain level of success could probably sing a song constructed out of the Yellow Pages and still have hits.

To be fair, there are also many obscure and complex songs that are simply boring and unlistenable. I don't find that obscurity is any guarantee of song quality. And some complex lyrics, like Don McLean's "American Pie," have become giant hits as well. The listener is the final arbiter of whether a song has an audience. There are always going to be writers whose work may be moderately successful but whose outstanding craft appeals more to other songwriters or musicians than to the general public. Kenny G. sells far more records than the late John Coltrane ever did; that doesn't make Kenny a better sax player. It is just that the music he records is simply more accessible to the average person. Writers like Jesse Winchester, Guy Clark, Mickey Newbury and the late Townes Van Zandt have all had some commercial success, but their work is best known by their peers rather than the general public.

TASTE AND CLICHÉS

I once had a bitter argument with my friend John Braheny about a song by Dan Hill, which had the lines in it "sometimes when we touch, the honesty's too much." John thought this to be a brilliant lyric, and I thought it was a rather sappy cliché. There is no right or wrong opinion to have in this sort of discussion. It is a question of taste, and I suppose if a psychiatrist got into the argument he would question exactly why we each had rather strong reactions to a fairly neutral notion.

In the same way I have never cared for Eric Clapton's song "Tears In Heaven," although millions of people bought this record and probably loved the song. From my point of view, the song was simply too autobiographical. It told me more about this particular tragedy in Clapton's life than I cared to know.

I am not maintaining that my view here is the correct one, I am simply making the point that one person's cliché may be another person's insight. What seems vapid to you may touch the heartstrings of millions of people.

CHAPTER 18 RESOURCES

I have drawn considerable inspiration and insight from Bill Flanagan's book *Written in My Soul: Conversations with Rock's Greatest Songwriters.* It was published in 1987 by Contemporary Books, and may be difficult for you to locate. Try your library. There are several other collections of interviews with songwriters listed in the appendix to this book.

What Others Do: Developing Your Analytical Skills

It is a good idea to look at the way other writers work. Every writer has periods of vulnerability and self-doubt, and it is best that you not choose those periods of your life to examine the works of other people in depth. This can result in your imitating other writers or writing styles, or it may make you doubt the validity of your work.

There are two basic ways to examine the work of other writers. One is to buy or borrow songbooks, and the other is to listen to recorded work. The trouble with songbooks is that seeing a songwriter's work on the printed page tends to freeze that work away from the music. It becomes an exercise similar to reading poetry. When you listen to recordings you can get a picture of how a song actually sounds. You can play through a song from a piece of sheet music, but unless you are a fairly skilled musician you may devote too much attention to reading the music and not enough to evaluating it.

FAKE BOOKS

Several music publishers, especially Hal Leonard Corporation, the publishers of this book, put together what are called "fake books." A fake book is a collection of songs generally reduced to a simply melody line (or lead sheet), chords and lyrics. The chords in fake books are usually somewhat simplified. This is done so that even a moderately trained musician can perform songs readily on what musicians call casuals or general business gigs, like weddings and functions.

Fake books are available in most musical genres. *The Ultimate Country Fake Book,* for example, includes more than seven hundred songs written by such prominent country writers as Harlan Howard, Bob McDill, Kostas and Kye Fleming.

Similar books cover jazz tunes, old standard pop tunes, rock songs, Latin tunes, etc.

WHAT CAN YOU LEARN?

Each genre of music has certain lyrical and musical mannerisms that are specific to that style. Obviously you could fill a large book with a critical analysis of song texts, rhyme schemes, point of view, melodies and chord progressions. It's worth a brief look, and I'll risk some broad generalizations to try to pin down some of these tendencies.

COUNTRY MUSIC

There are two contradictory lyrical trefnds that turn up over and over in country music. One stylistic mannerism is to celebrate carousing. Such songs talk about men or women (usually the former, even today) who cheat on their spouses, drive trucks, drink beer, and in general raise hell. I suppose that Hank Williams Jr. personifies this sort of attitude.

Another sort of song celebrates faithfulness and spiritual, religious or patriotic values, and in general advocates a more traditional lifestyle.

More recently writers like Mary Chapin Carpenter and Lyle Lovett have presented a more complex and sophisticated view of life, and their songs tend to call attention to odd situations. These writers definitely offer a more progressive sort of social commentary than is found in the work of more mainstream country writers.

In any case, the majority of country songs tell coherent stories. They often follow a particular character throughout the song. The melodies tend to be somewhat repetitious and relatively simple. There are comparatively few country songs where the listener can't sing along with the recording. The chord progressions are also relatively easy to play, and most amateur musicians will be able to play along by ear.

Wordplay, especially in the title of a song, can be a very important element in country music. Some good examples of this sort of title include "All My Exes Live In Texas," "Feelin' Single, Seeing Double," or "If I Said You Had A Beautiful Body Would You Hold It Against Me?"

A few of the many talented country writers whose work you may want to examine include Harlan Howard, Bob McDill, Kostas, Willie Nelson and, of course, Hank Williams (the father, not the son).

On the next page are the words and music of a song that I wrote and recorded, entitled "Soon You Will Be Coming Back to Me." As we discussed in the bluegrass section, the lead is sung in the tenor register, and another vocal is above it. The singers are Tim and Mollie O'Brien, and the lead instruments are fiddle and banjo. This song was used in the 2009 season of the NBC-TV show "My Name Is Earl."

POP STANDARDS

Pop standards are songs that generally stem from the period from 1930 to 1950. The writers are people like Jerome Kern, Richard Rodgers, Lorenz Hart, Oscar Hammerstein, George and Ira Gershwin, Harold Arlen, Cole Porter, Leigh and Coleman, and later, Stephen Sondheim. Except for Sondheim, all of these writers are dead. The style survives, to an extent, in the work of such writers as Burt Bacharach. In general, Broadway and Hollywood are the last strongholds of this musical style. Writers like Jule Styne, Robert Merrill, Johnny Mercer, Henry Mancini and Michael Masser are more modern examples of writers of this sort.

The authors of these standards prided themselves on sophistication and intelligence. They used a variety of poetic devices to do this. In his song "Another Op'nin', Another Show," Cole Porter rhymed *show* with *Baltimore*, owing to the colloquial pronunciation of "Baltimore." This is also the case with "April in Paris," where lyricist E. Y. Harburg "rhymes" *Paris* with *reprise*.

The music of the standards tends to be much more complex than what we find in other genres of popular music.

⟨43⟩ "Soon You Will Be Comin' Back to Me"

(by Dick Weissman)

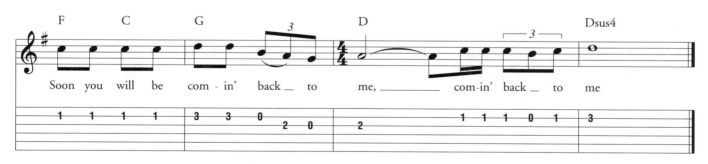

The chord progressions require the musician to have a higher technical knowledge of music, often utilizing such devices as diminished and augmented chords, extended chords that utilize bass pedal points, and so forth. Because of this musical complexity, many jazz musicians have taken standards and developed complex instrumental improvisations based on them. John Coltrane's lengthy expansion of the Rodgers and Hammerstein song "My Favorite Things" is one example.

ROCK 'N' ROLL

There have been so many wonderful songwriters in the world of rock 'n' roll that it is difficult to know whom to include and whom to leave out in a brief discussion. Chuck Berry, Buddy Holly, Gerry Goffin and Carole King, Bob Dylan, John Lennon and Paul McCartney, Van Morrison, David Byrne, Stevie Wonder, Neil Young; the list goes on and on. It isn't a bad idea for an aspiring writer to examine the Beatles' music in its entirety.

What rock brought to the songwriting table was high-voltage energy, fun and a willingness to write about almost anything. The pop standards of the '40s and '50s tended to focus on unrealistic fantasy-driven romances or novelty songs. Chuck Berry and Buddy Holly brought in aspects of everyday life, especially the life of teenagers.

The Beatles and Bob Dylan opened up whole new subject areas, song techniques and ways of expressing thoughts and feelings. Dylan brought the run-on sentences so popular in the work of Beat novelists and poets like Jack Kerouac and Alan Ginsberg to popular music. He wrote about nuclear holocausts, racial injustice, failed romances, bad men of the Old West, religious experiences, and contemporary and historical figures of interest. The Beatles wrote

about places, old-time British vaudeville, lonely spinsters, romances, authors, nostalgia, and whatever suited them.

Dylan's music tends to be fairly simple, but the Beatles were more musically sophisticated. Besides their foundation in Little Richard, Chuck Berry and other early rock 'n' roll, they were partly influenced by George Martin and other styles of music and art, and incorporated touches of Indian music and a sophisticated use of electronics. They also wrote quite a few songs that used shifting rhythms, moving from one meter to another in mid-song. Somehow, they still retained the sense of youthful amusement and diversion that was so evident in the earlier days of rock 'n' roll.

Other sub-genres of rock 'n' roll have developed over the years, such as punk and heavy metal. Punk lyrics tend to be overtly rebellious and anti-establishment, and the music is relatively basic, with a lot of shouting over simple chord progressions. Heavy metal can range from an exaggerated version of hard rock to the hardcore punk hybrid of speed metal and the dirgelike stylings of death metal, with appropriations from fusion, classical, techno and, more recently, rap, thrown in along the way. The lyrics tend toward anti-establishment, macho posturing, and the music often features chords without thirds, as discussed earlier. These chords are termed "power chords."

We have included two rock songs on the CD. The first is "Cry Love," coauthored by Tony Rosario and Jim Mason. The song is printed here, exactly as it was given to me. As with many rock songs, notice how crucial the production is to getting across the message of the song. Notice how few chords are used in this piece, and how seldom they change. This greatly contributes to the moodiness of the song.

◆ ④ "Cry Love"

Words and music by Tony Rasario/Jim Mason
I Knew That Publishing, BMI and Takeabyte Music
    Publishing ASCAP. Used by permission

Verse 1

F♯m
You get angry at the madness that comes
        knockin' at your door.
You're tryin' to be stronger,
        wishin' you were more.
Your heart's grown cold and distant,
        and your hope is almost gone,
Your friends all act like strangers,
        a change is coming on.

CHORUS

B
Cry love, Cry love.

B
Cry love, Cry love.

Verse 2

You know love can move a mountain,
        love can part the sea,
It can deal the deepest heartache,
        its power sets you free.
It's stronger than the mighty,
        it's older than the stars,
It's the proof that there's a heaven,
        it'll find you where you are.

Next is another rock song, this one is more in a '50s style. The song is entitled "Like You Never," and it was written by Grant Landsbach, and is used with his permission. It is performed by his group, the Lindys. There are three parts to the song; note the unusual form, with a sort of double chorus.

◆ ④ "Like You Never"

Words and music by Grant Landsbach

A1

Oh back when I was young.
And all I really cared for was my fun.
You said, "Boy why you lookin' at me?"
I said, "I don't know, I guess I just like what I see."

B1

And all along the fences we would sit,
And talk about our dreams and what they meant
And vowed to live a life without regrets... without regrets.

C1

And you'd say, "Wait a minute, I don't wanna get in the
        middle of it
I just wanna, I just wanna have fun."
You'd say, "Wait a minute I don't wanna get in the
        middle of it
I just wanna, I just wanna, have fun."
I'd say, "I don't think I've ever had a girl like you,
        yes and no one's ever done it like we're gonna do."

A2

So goodbye to the times as a child,
And I can look back but it took me awhile.
And goodbye oh to the things I know,
I've spent one too many nights with the late night show.

B2

'Cause all along the fence we would sit,
And talk about our dreams and what they meant,
And vowed to live a life without regrets... without regrets.

C2

And you'd say, "Wait a minute I don't wanna get
        in the middle of it
I just wanna, I just wanna have fun.'
You'd say, "Wait a minute I don't wanna get in the
        middle of it
I just wanna, I just wanna have fun."
I'd say, "I don't think I've ever had a girl like you,
        Yes and no one's ever done it like we're gonna do."

FUNK AND SOUL

In my opinion, you can't go wrong studying the works of Curtis Mayfield. His subject matter was the everyday world of the African-American. Love, prejudice, prison, obstacles to freedom, Greek myths, junkies and lovers were all grist for Curtis' lyric-writing mill. Mayfield had a strong poetic bent, and lines like "If there's any good in me, I want to bring it out so that you can see" or "It's hard to understand, there was love in this man" are simple ways of expressing complex ideas. The first line is sung by a man in prison who is missing his lover in the song "I Can't Wait Any Longer." The other line is from Mayfield's score to the film *Superfly*, specifically the song "Freddie's Dead."

Other writers in this style include James Brown, Otis Redding, Booker T. Jones, Steve Cropper, Dan Penn and Spooner Oldham. By far the leading subject of soul music is failed or unrealized romance. There are lots of minor seventh and ninth chords, with relatively simple chord progressions.

There is an aspect of soul music that is difficult to glean from books, and even from recordings. The impact of the song is heavily tied in to the transmission of emotion. In my opinion this emotional expression is probably more important than any other specific aspect of the music. Many soul lyrics seem relatively cold and not all that interesting when consigned to paper. But when they are sung by a master of the trade, like Aretha Franklin, the songs seem to take on much greater significance.

Only a broad exposure to the styles, together with an understanding of the origins, culture and development of the music, can really transmit the essence of soul.

FOLK

There are a number of excellent writers who are folk-oriented or derive their inspiration from folk music. Joni Mitchell, Bob Dylan, Neil Young, Tracy Chapman, James Taylor and Pete Seeger are all significant folk-oriented songwriters.

Joni Mitchell is superb at capturing the complexities of romance and the contradictory feelings that a love relationship inspires. At the same time some of her best songs are as much philosophical as they are personal. "Urge for Going" and "The Circle Game" in particular are songs about loneliness, restlessness and the life cycle that all human beings endure. What other writer would refer to her own persona as "like a cactus tree, so busy being free"?

Pete Seeger is often thought of more as a godfather of American folk music—a man who can make the coldest audience sing along—than as a writer. Yet among the songs he has written or co-authored are "If I Had a Hammer," "Kisses Sweeter Than Wine" and "Turn, Turn, Turn." The works of both Seeger and Michell have been compiled in large songbooks, so they are easy to study.

The music of folk or folk-pop tends to be somewhat similar to country music, but is a bit less formulaic. It draws on the same southern Appalachian, Scottish-Irish-English roots that shaped country and western music, but it also is influenced by African-American and world music styles.

There are a number of younger writers, like Conor Oberst and Sufjan Stevens, whose work has been influenced by folk music.

RAP

My friend Ted Myers, until recently an A&R producer at Rhino Records, refers to rap as a sound collage rather than a traditional form of songwriting. I take it that he is describing the use of rhythmic grooves, samples from existing records, and DJ turntable techniques that are used in dance clubs as well as on recordings.

As with soul music, rap is inextricably tied to a series of cultural events and historical developments. Without some comprehension of these roots and branches, it is difficult to become integrated into the rap family tree. The music really requires a grasp of MIDI and the construction of drum beats, and an inexorable emphasis on the groove of a song. Traditional melody as we know it is not a part of rap, although in the past few years different musical styles have been integrated into rap as a result of its tremendous popularity and energy.

Rap lyrics constitute street poetry. The subjects range from romance to violence to social protest. A good, if dated, collection called *Rap the Lyrics* is a reasonable tour guide into the idiom. As much as social critics have excoriated the lyrics of rap, especially the gangsta variety, it is remarkable to me that few critics have praised the clever wordplay and inventive use of language and poetic form in many rap songs. The run-on sentences with ad-lib rhymes really have much in common with the more free-flowing songs that Bob Dylan has written from time to time.

UNCLASSIFIED

Many critics enjoy stereotyping songwriters or artists. Often the most interesting artists are a mélange of different musical and lyrical styles. Today the music of virtually the entire world is available on disc, and ultimately, over the Internet. It is no wonder that so many "foreign" influences have come into play.

My friend John Phillips, founder of the Mamas and Papas, is often typecast as a folk-rock writer. In fact his influences include jazz vocal groups like the Hi-Los, country and western music, folk music, show tunes, rhythm and blues, and virtually every other musical style extant. Because I have known John for many years, I am aware of his many unrecorded songs, not just the many hits enjoyed by the Mamas and Papas, such as "California Dreamin',"

"Monday, Monday," "Creeque Alley," etc., etc. Even on the group's albums John would occasionally include such gems as "Strange Young Girls," a lyrical description of the acid-drenched flower-power ladies of the canyon.

There is currently no collection in print of John's songs, but having cowritten with him and observed his song process for some years, I think I can describe it in a useful way.

John starts out with a basic thread of an idea, starts to create some guitar lines, and then reworks the song until he is satisfied with it. He generally likes to work at night and, in my experience, does most of his rewriting during a process that goes on for several hours.

THE INTELLIGENCE FACTOR

Because John Phillips was a very intelligent person, his songs tend to spill over into many lyrical and musical styles and gestures. The truth is that there are quite a few capable hit songwriters who do not share his broad interests, and whose songs always reflect that set of limitations. In my judgment, one of the key factors in songwriting is to go beyond the limits of your own experiences. If a writer is not limited by his own social world or history, then he will be able to maintain a career that can last as long as he is capable of seeing and hearing other people's realities.

INSTRUMENTAL MUSIC

Instrumental music will never be as profitable as lyrical songs, but it can be extremely satisfying to both the writer and the listener. It has its own strengths, limitations and challenges. For many people, music without words is simply an abstraction that they cannot understand. If they do comprehend it is often because the music has been delivered in the broadest strokes and in the most obvious way. On the other hand, for some listeners, this "limitation" is exactly what they like about it. Since there are no words, listeners can invent their own mood, and interpret the sounds in whatever way they find gratifying or interesting.

Some instrumental writers have a tendency to limit this free-flowing reaction by imposing very specific titles on their music. If I entitle a piece "After the Columbine Massacre," I am pretty much telling the listener what he is supposed to feel. For this reason I generally try to come up with titles for instrumental music that are less specific.

Instrumental music can be studied both from recordings and from folios. Such guitarists as Leo Kottke, Pierre Bensusan and John Renbourn have books of their solos available, as do pianists such as George Winston or Dick Hyman. Instrumental music is also often used in movie scores or commercials.

Because instrumental music is playable in as many genres as the songs we have discussed, it would take up considerable text here to detail each instrumental genre. New age and new acoustic music are two genres of music that are primarily instrumental rather than song-driven. New age music tends to be repetitious and hypnotic. Some listeners find it soothing and healing, others are bored by it. New acoustic music is music that incorporates ingredients of folk, country and jazz instrumental technique. Artists like Dave Grisman and Tony Rice perform their own compositions in this style. It is essentially a category without category. The only rule is that by definition the music is acoustic rather than electric.

◆ 46 "Pioneer Nights"

On the CD I have included an original guitar piece of

mine, entitled "Pioneer Nights." It is the title cut from my new album on the Wind River label. It is included by permission of Wind River, and of Long Bridge Music Publishing, ASCAP.

I have deliberately not provided any music for this tune, which has a number of different sections, and is written in the key of G.

JAZZ

Jazz is primarily an instrumental style, and entire books have been written about the different subgenres of this type of music. These include Dixieland, swing, bebop, fusion and avant-garde styles. Once again, instrumental fake books and instructional materials are readily available if you want to expand your knowledge of jazz instrumental styles.

CHAPTER 19 RESOURCES

Songbooks by the Beatles, Bob Dylan, Joni Mitchell and many of the other artists mentioned are readily available.

The Hal Leonard Corporation Fake Book referred to in this chapter is the fourth edition of *The Ultimate Country Fake Book*. Other fake books and songbooks are listed in the appendix of this book.

The rap lyric collection is entitled *Rap: The Lyrics; The Words to Rap's Greatest Hits.* It was published in 1992 by Penguin Books. A newer collection is *Hip Hop and Rap: Complete Lyrics for 175 Songs*, published by Hal Leonard in 2003.

More Opportunities and Resources for Songwriters

SONGWRITERS' ORGANIZATIONS

NSAI is the dominant national songwriters' organization at this time. They have offices in Nashville that contain writers' rooms, a library, and administrative offices. NSAI also has branches in a number of states that offer reduced, local versions of the events sponsored in Nashville. The events sponsored at the home office include intensive workshops with leading songwriters and publishers, and classes that meet on a regular basis. The "outreach services" include cosponsoring song critiques and publisher-songwriter visits to outlying areas.

The advantage of affiliation with this network is that in most parts of the country the only thing available is local songwriters' organizations. We will discuss these groups in more detail below. It is invaluable to listen to people who are active in the business describing what the current practices of the business are. In addition, these meetings often provide song critiques by the visiting lecturer or lecturers.

SONG CRITIQUES

If you have never had a song critiqued in public, it is probably useful to read over the following description of that process. The publisher comes to a city where they know few, if any, writers. The songwriters' group usually arranges for a certain number of songs to be played for the publisher, who then describes his or her immediate reactions. The selection process may be a filtering or weeding-out process sponsored by the local group, or it may be done on a first come, first served basis. The other possibility is a sort of ad-lib roulette, where the songs are randomly selected in some fashion. At the old Los Angeles Songwriters Showcase, they actually placed the tapes on a roulette wheel and spun the wheel. A very California solution.

It is best if the publisher doesn't actually know who wrote the song at the time he hears it. This ensures that the publisher will not have any positive or negative prejudices toward the writer.

WHAT TO EXPECT

The publisher listens to the song and looks at a lyric sheet or lead sheet while the song is playing. In most instances the publisher will listen to the first verse and the chorus. Unless the publisher immediately gets excited about the song, he will then usually stop the tape and make comments.

You may be upset by such a peremptory listening session. Under these conditions he publisher is generally looking for:

1) Great choruses.
2) An intriguing title.
3) A first verse that makes him want to hear more.

Most songs are not going to fulfill all of these criteria. Consequently the publisher will then go on to listen to the next song. Don't beg the publisher to listen further. He has already concluded that the song isn't suitable for publication at this time.

If the publisher really likes a song, he will then ask to talk to the writer. Often the publisher will ask to take the song home to listen to it again in the office. This doesn't necessarily mean that the writer will be offered a deal, but it at least means that from here on in the writer will have an open door to that publisher. In some circumstances the publisher will then ask the writer to send more songs in. This may result in a staff writing relationship, or it may simply mark the beginning of a relationship that will ultimately lead to a staff writer deal.

The bad news is that often the publisher will take the song home and then conclude that it is a good song, but not one that is worthy of investing his time and money to promote and publish.

LOCAL SONGWRITING ORGANIZATIONS

In my opinion you should seek out and join any local songwriting organizations that you can find. They can provide you with a number of opportunities. These can include:

1) Hooking you up with possible collaborators.
2) Getting your songs critiqued by people who have similar objectives to your own.

3) Sponsoring either occasional guest lectures by national or regional professionals, or even sponsoring regional music conferences, described below.
4) Providing a source for the exchange of services between singers, writers, musicians and recording studios. Through this exchange you can lower your cost in making demos.
5) Offering a support group. Although the quality of the writers may vary, the goals of most of the members are similar: to get their songs recorded.

THE DOWNSIDE

The downside of local songwriting or music organizations is that they provide limited professional opportunities. Boise isn't Los Angeles, and Shreveport isn't Nashville. If you are a hard-working writer with a professional attitude, you may well find that the low quality of other writers' work is depressing and even inhibits your own enthusiasm for writing. There are thousands of people who are writing or trying to write songs, and for some of them it's a hobby rather than a serious pursuit.

It can also be dangerous to have your work critiqued by people who don't know what they are talking about. The experience, talent and sophistication level of a local organization may not be sufficient to provide much stimulation for you. If this happens repeatedly, you should probably consider moving to a larger music market.

It is possible to live outside the major music markets and still maintain an active writing career. In order to do so you will have to figure out a way to access these markets. This can be done through a publisher based in a major market, or through regular trips to major markets. Another book of mine, *Making a Living in Your Local Music Market,* also published by Hal Leonard Corporation, tackles these issues in great detail.

REGIONAL MUSIC CONFERENCES

Sometimes regional music conferences will include time for song critiques. Even when they don't, publishers and writers often attend these meetings. It is always worthwhile to establish initial contacts with publishers or performing rights organizations in such situations. If the contact goes well, a publisher who normally does not accept unsolicited material may reveal a code that will get your tape package past the secretaries and avoid you the annoyance of receiving your envelope with "UNSOLICITED MATERIAL NOT ACCEPTED" on it.

CRITIQUING SERVICES

There are some songwriters and companies that will critique your songs in return for a fee. The best known of these is a Los Angeles firm called TAXI. I have to confess that I have some misgivings about paying someone to listen to songs. If you do decide to go this route you need to know:

1) Who is going to listen to your work? The phrase "experienced industry experts" doesn't necessarily mean anything.

2) Is the listener someone who is up to date with current market practices, and has a direct connection with A&R staff, producers, publishers and artists? It may be that the listening staff is perfectly competent, but that their knowledge of the business is not up to date in the particular musical style in which you write.

3) Exactly what services will be provided to you? Will there be a written critique? How specific and detailed is it going to be?

4) If the service says that it will hook up the qualified writers to publishers or producers, is there going to be an additional fee for that networking? If there IS an additional fee, this may be an indication that

the company or writer is earning a good income for these services, but that you are just a pawn in their game.

5) How quickly will you get a response to your work? A few weeks is reasonable; three or four months isn't. Styles change, and so will the value of the critique if it takes too long.

6) Is the company listening to your song going to try to control your publishing rights in return for their services?

SONGWRITING CONTESTS

Billboard magazine, music festivals and other groups sponsor songwriting contests. The prizes vary from a considerable amount of cash to free recording time, or musical or technical support supplies. As usual, there are pros and cons in dealing with these opportunities.

The Kerrville Folk Festival in Texas and the Telluride Bluegrass Festival have contests that include public performances. They are most advantageous for singer-songwriters, and not very useful if you are not a good singer or performer. Winning these contests results in a paid gig the following year performing in front of thousands of people. This can represent a valuable opportunity.

The contests that *Billboard* sponsors are much larger. There are entry fees, and hundreds if not thousands of people enter. There are professional judges, but picture yourself listening to dozens and dozens of songs in a relatively brief time span. I also must admit that I tend to be opposed to contests that require entry fees.

My favorite contest story is one about a Denver writer named Bobby Allison. He won the $50,000 Marlboro Writer-Performer contest. In addition to the cash prize, he received a recording contract with Sony. He went to Nashville to meet his "producer," who was on staff at Sony at the time. Bobby got a ten-minute audience, because the producer was about to drive to the airport to go somewhere else.

The recording session did take place and the record was released. Of course the record received no promotional help from Sony. Bobby spent quite a bit of his prize money hiring independent promoters in a vain attempt to breathe life into the record. It didn't work out, and that was the end of the story. Bobby, who is a talented singer-songwriter, now plays regularly at a club in Sturges, South Dakota.

IS THERE AN UPSIDE?

If you win a national contest, you can always place that on your résumé. You also may get a recording session, some money and some national exposure. My advice is that you shouldn't expect that even a victory in a national contest will provide any guarantee that you will then go on to national fame or fortune.

DECISIONS

The decision on whether to enter songwriting contests or pay money for song critiques is obviously yours. If you are totally without contacts in the music publishing or recording world, and if you have no ability to travel to the major music centers, it is probably worth considering.

Some of these contests are big money-making opportunities for the contest promoters. If 50,000 people enter songs (and many enter multiple songs), and it costs, for example, $10 for each song entered, the contest will gross $500,000 from these fees. If the prizes have a value of $100,000, and the cost of promoting the contest and hiring people to screen the songs adds another $50,000, the contest still makes a profit of $350,000. It also means there will be perhaps 10 winners and 49,990 losers.

Someone wins the lottery, but most people lose!

Before doing so, I would make sure that you have exploited any local contacts and anyone in the business whom friends, family, business associates, local concert promoters, performers, or disc jockeys might know. In my opinion any of those types of direct contacts are more apt to pay off than what I would see as the equivalent of playing the lottery.

OTHER OPPORTUNITIES FOR SONGWRITERS

As you become more experienced and your skills grow in songwriting and its associated music business aspects, there are a number of things that you can try to do to grow your career. This is particularly true if it is your goal to quit a regular day job and work full-time in music.

PLAYING OPPORTUNITIES

If you are a good musician or singer, it is possible to find work in a variety of contexts. Local music markets have many venues beyond the ones that you may be aware of. Many sections of the country have numerous conventions or regional meetings. Invariably the company or organization or sponsor of these events wants to hire live music to accompany their sales presentations. These jobs are generally gotten through chambers of commerce, catering services, local offices of the American Federation of Musicians, or booking agents who specialize in such events.

RECORDING

Similarly, there are recording studios in every part of the United States. Currently, through hard disc recording and ADAT formats, it is possible to set up a reasonable studio with relatively little expense. The sound quality in these "home studios" often surpasses what we used to think of as professional gear ten or twenty years ago.

Recording sessions done through union contracts pay quite well. If you are in the early phases of your career, you may prefer to look at the possibility of an exchange of services rather than seeing recording as a profit-making situation.

JINGLES

If you are a talented lyric writer, you may be able to get involved in writin g commercials on a local or regional level. In the largest cities this work is handled through independent music houses. They in turn deal with the advertising agency that handles a product. The agency deals directly with the company that makes the product. In smaller markets you will more likely deal directly with the advertising agency, because there isn't a lucrative enough local market to justify independent music houses.

DIVISION OF LABOR

If your local agency fancies themselves as talented lyricists, your role might be to write the music and produce it in a studio. Another method of working is for the agency to suggest certain key aspects of the lyric, or the name of the campaign. They will then rely on you to come up with the words and music of the jingle.

You should be paid a creative fee for writing the jingle, another fee for singing and/or playing, and yet another fee for recording the music in your own studio. Creative fees for local jingles are relatively modest, often in the $500-to-$1,000 range. When a jingle is a regional jingle these fees escalate, and national creative fees can run as high as $25,000 or even more.

It is quite advantageous for you to join the union and use union contracts, because commercials pay re-use fees, known as residuals, to singers and musicians. Under certain circumstances, based on the type and length of usage, singers can earn thousands of dollars from a single commercial. Often the vocal took only an hour or two to record.

In local markets the clients often would rather work non-union and pay a single fee, known as a buyout. This means that you receive one lump sum payment and never get any re-use fees. This is obviously not to your advantage as a singer or musician.

VIDEO GAMES, SLIDE SHOWS, LIBRARY MUSIC AND LOCAL CABLE TV

All these markets have opportunities for original music. The video games market is a relatively new phenomenon, but a growing one. As much time is being expended on this medium as on records. Slide shows usually require simple music backgrounds, and if you are a good keyboard player or guitarist, your music might fill the bill.

Music libraries license music for commercials, for film and television at relatively modest prices. They often license the same music for multiple uses. For example, a commercial for a bank in Dubuque, Iowa may also be used as a commercial for an automobile dealer in Tucson, Arizona. If it is instrumental music, there will simply be a different voiceover. If the jingle is sung, the same instrumental track will be used and the singers will sing a different lyric, appropriate for the use.

Because so many people have fairly well-equipped recording studios these days, music production libraries currently turn out a superior product to what they did, say, twenty years ago.

Local cable and network TV often needs filler music,

ranging in length from a few seconds to a few minutes. This fills the gap between shows. There is usually a modest one-time payment, and they can use the music whenever and however they wish.

However, unless you sign away the rights, you will also receive payment from the performing rights organizations whenever the music plays.

RECORD PRODUCTION

By producing demos you should be developing a knowledge base that can lead you into the area of record production. Many local bands require record production services, and so do national and international superstars. It is best never to produce any recordings without obtaining a production agreement that pays you a percentage of the retail sale of the recording. The percentage can range from 3% to 5%. As a beginner 2% might be a fair fee. In addition you should receive some sort of flat fee for rehearsing with the artist and spending the necessary dozens of hours in the recording studio. This fee is often considered to be an advance against royalties.

If you work for an hourly fee, without a royalty agreement, you will become very upset if the recording becomes successful. It is never possible to know exactly how successful a particular recording will be. I prefer not to work by the hour as a producer, because I regard an album as a unified project, with an overall process, rather than as a gig for a single night.

MOVIES

There are locally produced movies in many parts of the United States. There are two possibilities for marketing your skills in this context. The first is getting your songs in the film. The second possibility, if you have the musical skills, is to write film scores.

The budgets for locally produced movies tend to be small, so if you get such a gig, try to hold on to your own music publishing. If you do the work without being compensated, because the filmmaker is "only entering the film in contests," be sure that you have an agreement that you will be compensated for any use of the film that results in income for the maker of the film.

In Hollywood there are agents who represent film composers. When doing a film score, the composer is provided with cue sheets that are a specific time breakdown of all events in the film. If you are working in a local market, you get to do all of these timings yourself. The music budgets on a Hollywood film are in the hundreds of thousands, but in a local market your entire music budget will probably be under $25,000, including your composing fee.

LAWYERS

Before you sign a contract with a music publisher, an advertising agency or the producer of a film, you should consult an entertainment business attorney. A national organization called Volunteer Lawyers for the Arts offers low-cost legal services.

If you consult a lawyer on your own, you can expect to pay $150 to $300 an hour for their services. It is sometimes possible, if negotiations become lengthy, to get a lawyer to agree to put a cap on his services. Under these circumstances you might reach an agreement that your legal services won't exceed, for example, $600.

SEMINARS AND CLASSES

There are a number of songwriting seminars and classes. Often they are offered through music festivals, such as the Kerrville Festival in Texas, or the Rocky Mountain Folk Festival in Lyons, Colorado. The value of these seminars depends upon the quality of the teacher, and the unpredictable chemistry that occurs in any classroom situation where a teacher and a group of students get together. It is amazing how the presence of one or two particularly enthusiastic or negative people can affect a learning environment. I have seen this happen time after time in the fifteen years that I have been teaching songwriting and music business classes at the University of Colorado at Denver and at Portland Community College.

It is also true that some really talented writers may turn out to be terrible teachers. By the same token some people who may not themselves be great writers have the ability to analyze and appreciate songs in an inspiring way. Try to find out as much as you can about the teachers of the class or seminar you are investigating, and if you decide to take the class, come in with a positive attitude. Later on you can evaluate whether you think the class has been a useful experience.

There is also a sort of "classroom junkie" personality. These people take every class known to exist, and often come in with the attitude that they know more than you do. Take it in stride and try to ignore it. The class isn't a personality contest, but a learning experience.

CHAPTER 20 RESOURCES

Many of the issues discussed here are dealt with in detail in my book *Understanding the Music Business*, Prentice-Hall, 2010.

Conclusion

We've looked at virtually every aspect of songwriting during the course of this book. The words, the music, the business of getting songs recorded, modern innovations in technology; all of these facets have been addressed.

You should now be at the point where you can take everything written in the book and remember what is useful for you, and disregard what you feel doesn't work. Songwriting is a wonderful pursuit, and whether or not you are able to achieve commercial success, it's something that you can continue to do and enjoy for the rest of your life. I encourage you to experiment with different writing techniques, musical genres and subjects. You will certainly experience periods of discouragement when you wonder whether it is even worth it to continue to write.

As long as you have a sense of joy and accomplishment in what you are writing, then you should continue to do it. Keep an open mind and an open ear, mixed with a healthy dose of skepticism. Try working with different collaborators and in different places. Write in your head, write with the guitar, write with the piano. Whatever you do, keep writing and listening to the writers who inspire you, wherever you may find them. With all of the musical genres and sub-styles that exist today, there's always room for excellence if you can find your proper niche. Good luck!

CHAPTER 21 RESOURCES

The appendix of this book contains further information on chord progressions, a beginner's guide to reading music and a list of books, songwriters' organizations and other resources intended for your use and information. Use it!

A BRIEF GUIDE TO MUSIC NOTATION

Reading music notation is one way to communicate with other musicians. From my point of view it is simply a tool. The same things can be accomplished by the use of your ear, but notation is a form of shorthand that enables quicker communication. There are numerous books that detail the principles of music notation. The purpose of this section is to encourage you to consult them.

THE MUSICAL STAFF

Notes are written on a musical staff, shown below. Piano players read notes in both the treble and the bass clefs, but guitar notation is only printed in the treble clef.

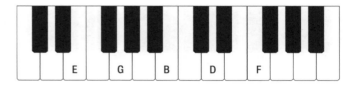

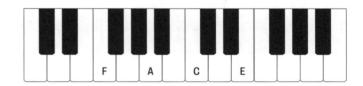

The names of the notes are written on the lines and spaces of the staff. The lines are written EGBDF (it is often memorized through the saying "Every good boy does fine"); the spaces spell out the word FACE. I have diagramed all of these notes on the piano keyboard and guitar tablature. Notes are also written above and below the musical staff, but they are a bit more difficult to read.

SHARPS AND FLATS

The sharp raises the pitch of a note a half step (C to C♯), while the flat lowers it a half step (A to A♭). The distance of one fret on the guitar is the same thing as a half step. This is shown in the diagram below. The musical symbol for sharps is ♯, and ♭ indicates a flat (C♯, A♭.)

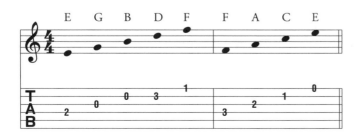

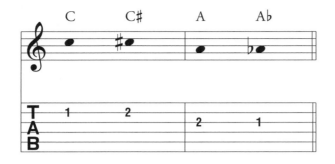

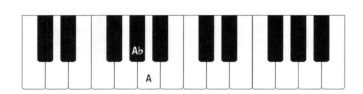

The sharps and flats are indicated in the key signature, which appears just after the G clef sign at the beginning of a piece of music. The key of G has one sharp, F♯. if you want a musician to play an F natural, you indicate this by placing a natural sign right next to the F note. This occurs often in blues songs.

Natural Sign

RHYTHM

The rhythm is indicated immediately after the sharps and flats. A rhythm of $\frac{4}{4}$ means that there are four quarter notes for each bar of music played; $\frac{3}{4}$ indicates that there are three quarter notes for each bar of music. When you

want a musician *not* to play a note, you indicate this with rest signs.

Rest Signs: Quarter, Half & Whole Rests

Below are the piano notes diagrammed on the keyboard. On the guitar diagrams I have indicated the notes through the fifth fret of the guitar. Note that C♯ and D♭ are the same pitch.

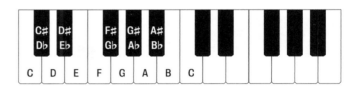

The bass or F clef of the piano is read differently. The F note is indicated by the space between the two dots in the clef symbol. Each note is a minor third (three frets) higher than it is in the treble clef.

This is obviously a very sketchy attempt to introduce music notation. There are many books that teach music notation; one that I like is *What Makes Music Work,* by Philip Seyer, Allan Novick and Paul Harmon, published by Seyer Associates in 1981. Guitar players may prefer any one of dozens of publications that specifically teach music notation for guitar.

◆47 CHORD PROGESSIONS

Finally, here are several additional chord progressions. I haven't diagrammed the chords here, but you can listen to them on the CD.

I VI II V7 I (In the key of C the chords are C A7 D7 G7 C.) This progression has a ragtime flavor, and can be found in a number of blues and bluegrass standards, such as "Keep On Truckin' Mama" and "Salty Dog."

I III7 IV I V7 I (In the key of C the chords are C E7 F C G7 C.) This is also found in a number of folk, ragtime and country tunes, such as "Railroad Bill" or "Make Me a Pallet on Your Floor."

Im ♭VII ♭VI V7 (In the key of Am the chords are Am G F E7.) This is the most popular chord progression in Spanish and Latin American music.

I major 7 to IV major 7 (In the key of C this is C major 7 to F major7.) This progression was frequently used by the band America, and Neil Young uses it in parts of several songs.

I IIm IIIm IV (In the key of C chords are C, D minor, E minor, F.) "Sunshine on My Shoulder," "The Best of My Love" and other songs use this progression.

For other information about chord progressions you can check out my own *Basic Chord Progressions,* published by Alfred Music, or a similar and more advanced book by Arnie Berle, published by Music Sales Corporation. Fake books are a great source of chord progressions.

OTHER MUSICAL RESOURCES

Following is a short list of books that deal with various musical matters.

Alexander, Peter. L. *More Songwriting and Composing Techniques.* Newbury Park: 1988, Peter L. Alexander Publishing. This book requires keyboard skills to be of any use.

Alternate Tunings Guitar Collection. (no author listed.) San Anselmo: String Letter Publishing, 2000. A selection by various artists, with a CD.

Coker, Jerry, Knapp, Bob and Vincent, Larry. *Hearin' the Changes: Dealing With Unknown Tunes by Ear.* No city listed, 1997. Jazz chord progressions.

Earnshaw, Mickey. *The Essence of Rhythm.* Fullerton: Centerstream Publishing, 1994.

Everett, Walter. *The Beatles as Musicians: Revolver Through the Anthology.* New York: Oxford University Press, 1999. An approach to music theory through the Beatles' music.

Fox, Dan and Weissman, Dick. *Fretboard Theory & Harmony.* New York: Schirmer Publications, 1985. A musical theory book for guitarists.

Hargrove, Bill and Ratcliff, Bob. *The Garage Band Method: How the Rest of Us Can Learn to Play.* Boise: Camel's Back Press, 1997. Garage band basics for rhythm sections.

Harrison, Mark. *Contemporary Eartraining, Level One and Level Two.* Milwaukee: Hal Leonard Corporation, 1994 and 1998.

Heatley, Michael and Alan Brown. *How to Write Great Songs: 100 Artists: All Styles.* London: Flame Tree Publishing, 2007.

Lilore, Joseph R. *The Songwriter's Guide to Chords and Progressions.* No city listed, 1982. Oriented toward keyboard players.

Phillips, Mark. *Understanding Rhythm.* Secaucus: Warner Brothers Publications, 1987.

Phillips, Hampton Peter. *The Rhythm Book*. New York: Dover Publications, 1995.

Rooksby, Rikky. *How to Write Songs on Guitar: A Guitar-playing and Songwriting Course*, second edition, Milwaukee: Backbeat Books, 2009.

Rooksby, Rikki. *How to Write Songs on Keyboards: A Complete Course to Help You Write Better Songs*. Backbeat Books, 2005.

Roseman, Ed. *Edly's Music Theory for Practical People*. Kennebunkport: Musical Ed Ventures, 1996. A logical approach to music theory, oriented toward the keyboard.

Scott, Richard. *Money Chords: A Songwrirer's Sourcebook of Popular Chord Progressions*. San Jose: Writer's Club Press, 2000.

Stewart, Dave. *Inside the Music. The Musician's Guide to Composition, Improvisation and the Mechanics of Music*. San Francisco: Miller Freeman Books, 1999. Fun to read, keyboard-oriented.

Seyer, Philip, Novick, Alan and Harmon, Paul. *What Makes Music Work*. Burlingame: Seyer Associates, 1982. Logical and intelligent, keyboard-oriented.

Silverman, Jerry. *A Folksinger's Guide to Note Reading and Music Theory*. New York: Oak Publications, 1966. Delivers what the title promises.

Weissman, Dick. *Guitar Tunings: A Comprehensive Guide*. New York: Routledge, 2006.

Wheaton, Jack. *101 Songwriting and Composing Techniques*. Newbury Park: Peter L. Alexander Publishing, 1987. Another keyboard-oriented book.

POETRY, RHYMES AND LYRICS

We have discussed the notion that songs are not poems in the early part of this book. However, in terms of following rhyme schemes and the length of lines, songs generally follow the forms used in poetry. Each line of a poem or a song is divided into feet, and each foot has syllables that are stressed. A number of books that discuss the form of poetry can provide you with detailed information about the names given to the various metrical lines and stresses.

Rhymes can come within lines or at the end of lines; there are also partial rhymes, called slant rhymes. It is a subject of argument among songwriters as to the importance of using true rhymes and having the length of lines relatively uniform. Of the four lines in a typical verse, a writer can rhyme lines 1 and 2, 3 and 4, or even 1 and 3 or 2 and 4. There are also songs that use rhymes in some verses and not in others.

Obviously the use of music influences the length of lines, and creative singers can stretch or constrict lyrics to go with music. It is also important to understand that the pronunciation of a word may differ. For example, take the word Oregon. Many people who live outside the state pronounce it as thought it were spelled Areegon. People who live in the state pronounce it as thought it were spelled Oreigin. The same confusion applies to such words as New Orleans. Locals pronounce it as thought it were spelled New Orlins, while outsiders (including songwriter Hal David in the song "Take This Message to Michael,") pronounce it like the actual spelling, New Or_leans._ When John Lee Hooker sang about Detroit he pronounced it with the emphasis on the first syllable, _De_. These variations in pronunciation don't just apply to geographic locations. Some people say ay-pricot, others say ahpricot for the word *apricot*.

If you listen closely to a number of songs, you will notice that the composer often slightly varies a melody from verse to verse, because the exact length of the lines in the verses may vary slightly. If this process becomes obvious, then it probably is not working efficiently.

Occasionally songs are written entirely without the use of rhymes, as in the standard "Moonlight in Vermont." Rhymes make songs easier to sing, but they may also lead to artificiality in the construction of lyrics. Everyone has heard songs whose lyrics seem almost entirely constructed with the aid of a rhyming dictionary.

Following are some books that will take you deeper into the forms of poetry. I have also included some books that particularly focus on the lyrics of songs.

POETRY BOOKS

Hobsbaum, Philip. *Metre, Rhythm and Verse Form.* London, Routledge, 1996.

Jerome, Judson. *The Poet's Handbook.* Cincinnati: Writer's Digest, 1980.

Oliver, Mary. *A Poetry Handbook.* San Diego: Harcourt, Brace, 1994.

Lyrics and Song Ideas

Aschmann, Lisa. *500 Songwriting Ideas (For Brave and Passionate People.)* Emeryville: Mix Books, 1997. A useful tool, especially if you've run out of ideas.

Bradley, Adam. *Book of Rhymes: The Poetics of Hip-Hop.* New York: Basic Books, 2009. An excellent guide to writing hip-hop lyrics.

Davis, Sheila. *The Songwriter's Idea Book.* Cincinnati: Writer's Digest Books, 1994. Ms. Davis has written several other books, but this one is particularly rich in ideas and exercises.

Mayfield, Curtis. *Poetic License.* Beverly Hills: Dove Books, 1996. The lyrics to a number of his great songs.

Mitchell, Joni. *The Complete Poems And Lyrics.* New York: Crown Publishing Co., 1997. Obviously there are many songwriters who deserve your attention, but Ms. Mitchell is a particularly brilliant lyricist.

Pattison, Pat. *Rhyming Techniques And Strategies.* Boston; Berklee Press, 1991. One of several books by Mr. Pattison. This is an extremely detailed book, and personally I find it a bit hard to follow.

Rimler, Walter. *Not Fade Away.* Ann Arbor: Pierian Press, 1984. A detailed comparison of Broadway and rock lyricists.

Stanley, Lawrence A., Ed. *Rap: The Lyrics. The Words to Rap's Greatest Hits.* New York: Penguin Books, 1992. A little out of date, but a great guide to the way rap lyrics are written.

Wilder, Alec. *American Popular Song: The Great Innovators, 1900-1950.* New York: Oxford University Press, 1972. A scholarly and detailed history of American popular song before rock 'n' roll.

RHYMING DICTIONARIES

The Merriam-Webster Dictionary is pocket-sized, and was published in 1995. *Rhyme Lines: The Rhyming Encyclopedia* is just that, and was published by Pendragon Publishing Ltd. in 1985.

Other rhyming dictionaries have been authored by Gene Lees and Sammy Cahn. Gene Lee's book is called *The Modern Rhyming Dicionary*, revised edition, published by Cherry Lane Music Company.

THE BUSINESS OF SONGWRITING AND MUSIC PUBLISHING

Dionne, Penny and Troy McConnell. *Songplugger: The Cuts and the Bruises*. Nashville: Nakita's Trail Publishing, 2008.

Editors, Writer's Digest Books. *2010 Songwriter's Market*. Cincinnati: Writer's Digest books, 2009.

Klavans, Kent J. *Protecting Your Songs & Yourself*. Cincinnati: Writer's Digest, 1989. Legal aspects of the songwriting business.

Koller, Fred. *How To Pitch And Promote Your Songs*. New York: Allworth Press, 1996. An excellent book for someone considering publishing their own music.

Mahonin, Valerie. *Market Your Songs*. Calgary: Songsmith Publications, 1986. A Canadian perspective, a bit dated.

NSAI. *The Essential Songwriter's Contract Book*. Nashville: NSAI, 1994. More about the legalities.

Pierce, Jennifer Ember. *The Bottom Line Is Money*. Westport: The Bold Strummer, 1994. The songwriting business in Nashville.

Poe, Randy. *The New Songwriter's Guide to Music Publishing*, third edition. Cincinnati: Writer's Digest, 2005. A well written, clear book.

Sobel, Ron and Dick Weissman. *Music Publishing: The Roadmap to Royalties*. New York, Routledge, 2008.

Southall, Brian with Rupert Perry. *Northern Songs: The True Story of The Beatles Song Publishing Empire*.

London: Omnibus Press, 2007. A detailed exploration of The Beatles' unfortunate adventures in the world of music publishing.

Whitsett, Tim. *Music Publishing: The Real Road to Music Business Success*, sixth edition. Emeryville: Music Pro Publishing, 2007. Another good book. More detailed, and a bit harder to read than the Poe book.

COMPREHENSIVE BOOKS ABOUT SONGWRITING

These books include material about lyrics, melodies and offer some coverage on the business of songwriting.

Appleby, Amy. *You Can Write A Song!* New York: Amsco Publications, 1991. A good beginner's guide.

Blume, Jason. *6 Steps to Songwriting Success: The Comprehensive Guide to Writing and Marketing Hit Songs*. New York: Billboard Books, 1999. A sensible and intelligent guide to commercial songwriting by a successful Nashville writer.

Braheny, John. *The Craft and Business of Songwriting*. Cincinnati: Writer's Digest, 1988. One of the first really good guides to commercial songwriting.

Citron, Stephen. *Songwriting: A Complete Guide to the Craft*. New York: William Morrow, 1985. A bit weak on the business aspects, but an excellent guide to lyric and melody writing.

Flanagan, Bill. *Written in My Soul: Conversations With Rock's Greatest Songwriters*. Chicago: Contemporary Books, 1987. A great book. Flanagan has an encyclopedic knowledge of songwriting and songs.

Gillette, Steve. *Songwriting and the Creative Process*.

Bethlehem: Sing Out, 1995. Gillette's text is excellent while articles by others vary in quality and usefulness.

Hirschhorn, Joel. *Songwriting: The Complete Idiot's Guide*, second edition. New York: Alpha Books, 2004. A much better book than the title implies.

Liggett, Mark and Cathy. *The Complete Handbook Of Songwriting*. New York: Penguin Books, Second Edition, 1993. A reasonable book, but not as useful as some of the others listed above.

Roach, Martin. *The Right To Imagination and Madness: An Essential Collection of Candid Interviews With Top UK Alternative Songwriters*. London: Independent Music Press, 1994. A useful supplement to Flanagan.

Schock, Harriet. *Becoming Remarkable: For Songwriters and Those Who Love Songs*. Nevada City: Blue Dolphin, 1999. Deals in depth with the emotional aspects of songwriting.

Sterling, Robert. *The Craft of Christian Songwriting*. New York: Hal Leonard Books, 2009. A useful guide to song construction, valuable even for writers who are not interested in the Christian music market.

Tucker, Susan, with Strother, Linda Lee. *The Soul of a Writer: Intimate Interviews With Successful Songwriters*. Nashville: Journey Publishing Co., 1996. Asks specific questions to a number of Nashville songwriters.

Waterman, J. Douglas, editor. *The Song: The World's Best Songwriters on Creating the Music That Moves Us*. Cincinnati: Writer's Digest Books, 2007.

Webb, Jimmy. *Tunesmith: Inside the Art of Songwriting*.

New York: Hyperion, 1998. Intelligent, opinionated and enjoyable.

Woodworth, Marc, Editor. *Solo: Women Singer-Songwriters in Their Own Words*. New York: Delta, 1998. Interviews with a number of interesting songwriters, well-known and otherwise.

Zollo, Paul. *Songwriters on Songwriting*, fourth edition. New York: Da Capo Press, 2003.

HISTORY OF SONGWRITING AND MUSIC PUBLISHING

Jasen, David A. & Jones, Gene. *Spreadin' Rhythm Around: Black Popular Songwriters, 1880-1930*. New York: Schirmer Books, 1998. A fascinating history.

Killen, Buddy. *By the Seat of My Pants: My Life in Country Music*. New York: Simon & Schuster, 1993. Great stories from a Nashville music biz pioneer.

Levy, Lester S. *Give Me Yesterday: American History in Song, 1890-1920*. Norman: University of Oklahoma Press, 1975. One of several books by this author that detail American history in song.

Read, Mike. *Major to Minor: The Rise and Fall of the Songwriter*. Surrey, U.K.: Biddles, 2000. The American and British Scene.

Shepherd, John. *Tin Pan Alley*. London: Routledge & Kegan Paul, 1982. A brief history of Tin Pan Alley.

Tawa, Nicholas. *A Music for the Millions*. New York: Pendragon Press, 1984. A survey of American popular music around 1850.

Tawa, Nicholas. *Sweet Songs for Gentle Americans: The*

Parlor Song in America, 1790-1860. Bowling Green: Bowling Green Popular Press, 1980. The story of parlor song and their singers.

Tawa, Nicholas. *The Way to Tin Pan Alley: American Popular Song, 1866-1910.* New York: Schirmer Books, 1990.

OTHER USEFUL BOOKS

Kislan, Richard. *The Musical: A Look at the American Musical Theater.* New York: Applause, 1995. A guide to the various aspects of writing and producing a musical.

Fisher, Jeffrey P. *How To Make Money Scoring Soundtracks and Jingles.* Emeryville: Mix, 1997. Fisher is practical and almost maniacally enthusiastic.

Notham, Mark and Miller, Lisa Anne. *Film and Television Composer's Resource Guide.* Milwaukee: Hal Leonard Corporation, 1998. A practical guide for composers in the business of film and television business.

Songwriter's Market. *The Songwriter's Market Guide to Song & Demo Submission Formats.* Cincinnati: Writer's Digest, 1994. How to submit demos, and where to send them.

Stone, Al. *Jingles: How to Write, Produce & Sell Commercial Music.* Cincinnati: Writer's Digest, 1990. A reasonable discussion of the jingle business.

ADDITIONAL BOOKS ABOUT THE BUSINESS OF SONGWRITING

Al and Bob Kohn's huge book *The Art of Music Licensing,* is an extremely detailed study of rights and legalities. It is published by Prentice Hall Law and Business Division, and is expensive but essential. Third edition, 2009.

Jeffrey and Todd Brabec's *Music Money and Success: The Insider's Guide to the Music Industry* has some really good breakdowns of income streams that a hit song can produce. Sixth edition, 2008.

OTHER RESOURCES: FAKE BOOKS, MAGAZINES, ETC.

Hal Leonard Corporation publishes a large selection of fake books, ranging from country to jazz to pop and even classical music. Warner Brothers Music has some good rock fake books, and Sher Music specializes in modern jazz fake books. Check your local music store for these books.

Another great source of musical and lyric ideas is *The Complete Beatles,* a two-volume set distributed by Cherry Lane Music.

Homespun Tapes has a series of cassette tapes called Songwriter's Workshop. The set includes tapes by Pat Alger, Fred Koller, Steve Gillete, Eric Kaz and John D. Loudermilk. There are six tapes, and they contain information about lyrics, piano and guitar accompaniments, and the business of songwriting. Write to Homespun Tapes, Box 694, Woodstock, New York 12498 for further information.

NSAI is the Nashville Songwriters Association Internat-ional. Its headquarters is at 1701 West End Ave., Nashville, TN 37203. They have branches in many parts of the country. Call 800-321-6008, send an e-mail to nsai@songs.org. or www.songs.org/nsai. They sponsor seminars and workshops, and have an extensive library and bookshop.

SGA Songwriters Guild of America/National Academy of Songwriters.

This organization is designed to protect songwriters. They offer sample contracts, and will collect royalties for a small percentage of what they collect. Their New York office is at 1560 Broadway, Suite, 1306, New York, NY 10036. 212-768-9047, SongNews@aol.com.

Their Los Angeles address is 6430 Sunset Blvd., Hollywood, CA 90028. LASGA@aol.com.

Their Nashville office is at 1222 16th Ave. South, Nashville, TN 37212. 615-329-1782, SGANash@aol.com. *Performing Songwriter* is an excellent monthly magazine that publishes articles about and interviews with songwriters. Subscriptions are available by calling 800-883-7664.

A more modest but still useful publication is *Songwriter's Monthly*. Subscriptions are available from 800-574-2986.

The United States Copyright Office offers free copyright forms by calling 800-366-2998.

Their web site is Icweb.loc.gov/copyright/

PEFORMING RIGHTS ORGANIZATIONS

ASCAP's web site is www.ascap.com. They have offices in Atlanta, Chicago, Los Angeles, Miami, Nashville and New York.

BMI's web site is www.bmi.com. They have offices in Atlanta, Los Angeles, Miami, Nashville and New York.

SESAC's web site is www.sesac.com, and they have offices in Nashville and New York.

Canadian writers should contact SOCAN. They can be reached by e-mail at socan@socan.ca. They have offices in Don Mills (a suburb of Toronto) Dartmouth, Nova Scotia, Edmonton, Montreal and Vancouver.